I'VE BEEN EVERYWHERE, MAN

A JOURNEY TO ALL THE PLACES IN AUSTRALIA'S FAVOURITE SONG

PETER C HARRIS

A QIQ PUBLICATION

I've been everywhere, man

First published 2025. A QiQ Publication.

PO Box 76, Malmsbury, Victoria 3446, Australia

Email: hello@peterharris.info

Website: www.ivebeeneverywhere.com.au

Copyright © Peter C Harris 2025

All rights reserved. No part of this publication may be reproduced, stored in a retrieval system or transmitted in any form or by any means — electronic, mechanical, photocopying, recording, or otherwise — without the prior written permission of the author, except in the case of brief quotations embodied in critical articles and reviews.

ISBN 978-1-7641431-6-5

A copy of this publication has been deposited with the National Library of Australia and the State Library Victoria in accordance with legal deposit requirements.

This is a personal travel memoir. The opinions expressed are entirely my own, based on my experiences at the time of travel. Historical events are recounted as part of Australia's rich and sometimes challenging past, and no criticism or disrespect is intended toward any community, individual or institution.

For my mum, who boarded her first plane for a long-haul flight to Australia at 85 — proof that it's never too late for an adventure. Your inspiration lives on.

CONTENTS

Prologue	1
1. The song that started it all	5
2. Geoff Mack: writer and composer	9

THE JOURNEY

1. Terrigal (NSW)	21
2. Kurri Kurri (NSW)	25
3. Gunnedah (NSW)	29
4. Narrabri (NSW)	33
5. Moree (NSW)	37
6. Boggabilla (NSW)	41
7. Goondiwindi (QLD)	43
8. Cunnamulla (QLD)	47
9. Augathella (QLD)	51
10. Morella (QLD)	55
11. Cloncurry (QLD)	59
12. Bambaroo (QLD)	65
13. Proserpine (QLD)	67
14. Gin Gin (QLD)	69
15. Wallaville (QLD)	71
16. Kumbarilla (QLD)	73
17. Brigalow (QLD)	75
18. Condamine (QLD)	77
19. Wallumbilla (QLD)	79
20. Muckadilla (QLD)	81
21. Bouindarra / Bundarra (NSW)/ Boroondara (VIC) *	83
22. Wyong (NSW)	87
23. Ettalong (NSW)	91
24. Tuggerawong (NSW)	95
25. Wollondilly (NSW)	99
26. Mittagong (NSW)	103

27. Brindabella (NSW)	107
28. Canberra (ACT)	111
29. Captain's Flat (NSW)	115
30. Jindabyne (NSW)	119
31. Ulladulla (NSW)	123
32. Unanderra (NSW)	127
33. Wollongong (NSW)	131
34. Gulgong (NSW)	135
35. Narromine (NSW)	139
36. Tullamore (NSW)	143
37. Molong (NSW)	147
38. Lithgow (NSW)	149
39. Megalong (NSW)	153
40. Kurrajong (NSW)	157
41. Turramurra (NSW)	161
42. Narrabeen (NSW)	165
43. Collaroy (NSW)	169
44. Kirribilli (NSW)	173
45. Woolloomooloo (NSW)	177
46. Caringbah (NSW)	181
47. Engadine (NSW)	185
48. Milperra (NSW)	189
49. Cabramatta (NSW)	193
50. Parramatta (NSW)	197
51. Girraween (NSW)	201
52. Boggabri (NSW)	205
53. Emmaville (NSW)	209
54. Wallangarra (QLD)	213
55. Dalveen (QLD)	217
56. Woodenbong (NSW)	219
57. Toowoomba (QLD)	221
58. Nambour (QLD)	225
59. Maroochydore (QLD)	229
60. Mooloolaba (QLD)	233
61. Strathpine (QLD)	237
62. Indooroopilly (QLD)	239
63. Yeerongpilly (QLD)	243
64. Coolangatta (QLD)	247

65. Tamborine (QLD)	251
66. Fingal (QLD)	253
67. Murwillumbah (QLD)	257
68. Mullumbimby (QLD)	259
69. Bangalow (NSW)	261
70. Lismore (NSW)	263
71. Casino (NSW)	267
72. Dorrigo (NSW)	269
73. Taree (NSW)	273
74. Stockinbingal (NSW)	275
75. Gundagai (NSW)	279
76. Adelong (NSW)	283
77. Jerilderie (NSW)	285
78. Billabong (VIC)	289
79. Yarra Yarra	293
80. Seymour (VIC)	295
81. Wangaratta (VIC)	299
82. River Murray (NSW)	303
83. Kilmore (VIC)	305
84. Dandenong (VIC)	309
85. Geelong (VIC)	313
86. Ballarat (VIC)	317
87. Bendigo (VIC)	321
88. Deniliquin (NSW)	323
89. Wanganella (NSW)	325
90. Grong Grong (NSW)	327
91. Darwin (NT)	329
92. Tibooburra (NSW)	333
93. Oodnadatta (SA)	341
94. Birdsville (QLD)	347
Epilogue	351
A - Z Index	353
Afterword	359
About the Author	363
Also by Peter C Harris	365

PROLOGUE

You know that feeling when life opens up a little window of freedom — when you realise you can step out of your usual routine and just... go?

That was me. I'd read *The 4-Hour Workweek* and actually put it into practice — no nine-to-five grind, no desk-bound obligations. I could work remotely when I needed to, laptop in one hand and coffee in the other, with nobody checking up on me.

At the same time, my partner — a former *MasterChef* contestant — was off chasing culinary adventures, leaving me at home with the dog and a choice: sit around waiting, or do something interesting.

So I thought: why not head off on a bit of an adventure? Not a carefully planned expedition — no spreadsheets, no rigid itinerary — just a rough idea to visit all the places made famous by that cracking old song, *I've Been Everywhere, Man*.

That song had always stuck in my mind — partly thanks to a brilliant old Telstra ad that made clever use of it, tapping into that idea of being able to connect from even the most remote corners of Australia. Somehow that ad planted the seed for this journey, years before I ever set off.

But it wasn't just about filling the time. I wanted to get to know Australia better — to really see this country. Not just the postcard spots, but the places few Aussies actually get to — those out-of-the-way towns where the pub might also serve as a post office and where kangaroos outnumber locals.

And that brings me to something that's hard to appreciate until you've seen it for yourself: just how *big* Australia is. Now, of course, "big" is subjective. I spent a good chunk of my life in the UK where, if you drive for four hours, you're in Scotland and it feels like you've crossed an entire country. In England, we think of places like Yorkshire as being "big". But England would fit into Australia nearly sixty times. Sixty! That's the scale we're talking about here — vast distances, long empty stretches, and a landscape that seems to go on forever.

My point is: it's almost impossible to comprehend just how large Australia actually is unless you start exploring it for yourself. But when something's so enormous... well, where do you even start?

For me, the song provided a handy list. So off I went. Not in one grand expedition but in stages — trips broken up with time back home, before heading out again. A mix of motels, road snacks, sunburnt dashboards and endless straight roads where it was just me, my dog Amelie (who was always up for extended walkies!), and a good podcast for company.

And how did it all wrap up? With a brilliant finale: rolling into Birdsville, way out there on the edge of the desert, with my mum (86 and still game for an adventure), my niece, my partner, and Amelie all along for the ride. A dusty, joyful gathering at the end of the road — the perfect way to finish a journey that was less about ticking off towns and more about soaking up the spirit of this vast, surprising, wonderful country.

Along the way, I even had the privilege of meeting Geoff Mack himself — the man who wrote *I've Been Everywhere* — and thanking him in person for the inspiration.

This book tells the story of that adventure.

CHAPTER 1
THE SONG THAT STARTED IT ALL

The history of *I've Been Everywhere, Man*

Long before Johnny Cash made it famous — and long before it became the unofficial anthem for grey nomads criss-crossing the outback — *I've Been Everywhere* started life as a humble cabaret opener.

In 1959, Australian songwriter Geoff Mack penned a tune he called *The Swagman Rock* — a rapid-fire roll call of Australian towns that made it perfect for cabaret. But it didn't really catch on until it got a new name and a new voice. Enter Lucky Starr: in January 1962, Starr's recording of *I've Been Everywhere* shot straight to number one on the Australian charts and stayed there for a remarkable fifteen weeks.

And that was just the beginning.

The original was quintessentially Australian, rattling off familiar place names in a breathless tongue-twister. But Mack's clever structure made it ripe for adaptation — and adapt it he did. Versions soon emerged tailored for audiences in the United States, New Zealand, Great Britain and Canada, all with lyrics rewritten (by Mack himself) to namecheck local towns.

Not content with a single hit, Lucky Starr doubled down, releasing an EP titled *Lucky's Been Everywhere*, with versions for Australia, the USA, Great Britain and New Zealand neatly packaged together (Festival Records FX-10.485 for the completists among us).

In the USA, the song took on a life of its own, reaching the top of the country charts in 1962 thanks to the smooth baritone of Hank Snow. Later versions would embed it firmly into pop culture, including the opening titles of the 2004 film *Flight of the Phoenix*.

And like any song that burrows its way into the collective imagination, *I've Been Everywhere* inspired countless covers — some earnest, some tongue-in-cheek. The list of artists who've taken a crack at it reads like a history of country music itself: Lynn Anderson, Johnny Cash, Asleep at the Wheel, Willie Nelson, The Statler Brothers and even The Sunny Cowgirls. There have been versions for New Zealand (John Grenell, 1966), Canada (Mike Ford, 2005), and the UK (Rolf Harris, 1963). There's even a parody version by the Farrelly Brothers for *The Aunty Jack Show* in 1974.

But perhaps the greatest testament to the song's universal appeal is the sheer number of niche adaptations it has inspired. There's an Alaska version, a Belgium version, one dedicated entirely to pubs, another dedicated (less tastefully) to pubic hair, and one wryly reworked for a *Simpsons* episode listing every Springfield in the United States.

Geoff Mack probably didn't imagine in 1959 that his little cabaret number would become a global template — endlessly adaptable, eternally catchy, and somehow still making people smile decades later.

In a way, *I've Been Everywhere* is itself a traveller — one of those rare cultural creations that just keeps going. It's not unlike the businesses we build: often humble in origin, opportunistic in adaptation, and sometimes — if you're lucky — capable of outliving even the person who set it in motion.

Must See

If you're keen for a musical pilgrimage, you can visit Tamworth, Australia's country music capital, where Geoff Mack is honoured as part of the Australian Country Music Hall of Fame — a fitting place for the song that's become a soundtrack to road trips across the country.

Fun Fact

The fastest performance of *I've Been Everywhere* was clocked at just under 2 minutes 30 seconds — but that's only possible if you barely take a breath! Lucky Starr himself once joked that you need a lungful of air and a good sense of humour to get through it live.

Key Statistics

- Written: 1959 by Geoff Mack

- First recorded: 1962 by Lucky Starr (Australia)

- Australian charts: No.1 for 15 weeks

- Countries with adapted versions: Australia, USA, UK, Canada, New Zealand... and counting!

- Most famous cover: Johnny Cash, 1996 (helped cement it as an anthem for American road trips)

CHAPTER 2
GEOFF MACK: WRITER AND COMPOSER

Shortly after I started my 'Everywhere' quest I decided to write to Geoff Mack, the writer and composer of I've been everywhere man, to see if I could get a further insight into his iconic lyrics. So I sent a mail off to some anonymous PO Box in Sydney and promptly forgot about it. However a couple of months later whilst visiting Gulgong, I was surprised and delighted to have a phone call from the gentleman himself when he kindly agreed I could visit. A couple of weeks and another phone call later and the meeting was set and I was now nervously strolling up his garden path.

Once at the door I pushed the bell but could not hear anything but I waited incase the bell was ringing in some far off corner of the property. Nothing happened so I tried the bell again, pushing a little harder and yes – the bell started to ring just the other side of the door. It rang... and rang and oh no... carried on ringing – I'd broken the bell push! As panic set in I tried pushing the bell push at different angles to stop it from ringing and from preventing the residents from thinking they had an impatient twit at the door holding the pusher. It was without success. Now, from the corner of my eye, I could see Geoff approaching with a stick! Fortunately Geoff took the incident all in his stride and after I asked for a screw driver, we soon had the bell fixed and I was advised it had never done that before. We then shook hands and Geoff led me in to his house, past his what I'll call his hallway of fame and into the kitchen where coffee was soon brewing and a tape with no less than 31 different versions of "I've been everywhere" (there is actually over 100) was set playing in the background.

Now, imagine filming the highlights of your life and storing the resulting film reels in your cupboard. How many reels would do you think you would have by the time you shoot your last scene – one, two, six or maybe a dozen? This question came to mind after Geoff proudly showed me his collection of 16mm film recordings of some of the highlights of his life. I did not count his reels but they easily filled a closet from top to bottom and reflect the full life Geoff has lived.

Geoff Mack

If there were a film in Geoff's film closet showing his birth it would be dated 20 December 1922 and shot in Surrey Hills, Victoria, Australia and it would not be long after this that Geoffs ability to entertain would soon be discovered. Geoff recalled to me how he was not the best pupil in the classroom (he described himself as a dud at school) with a relatively short attention span and recalled how a Sunday School parody of All things bright and Beautiful (which became "All things black and ugly, all slimy things that crawl, hooping cough and chicken pox the Lord God made them all") was not welcomed by his teachers. But the Great Depression was about to hit Australia and with it Geoff was moved in and out of school as parental funding allowed.

It makes you wonder what the impact of a global depression and then, within 10 years the Second World War would have on a young man such as Geoff Mack just setting out in life. I'd like to think that Geoff was a bright beacon in such dark times and his abilities to entertain and make people laugh were a highly regarded currency. Perhaps this is so, as it was not long after Geoff joined the RAAF in 1942 as a mechanic he was soon performing at concert parties, supporting Gracie Fields, and serving in Borneo and later Japan (Geoff can sing Old MacDonald's Farm in Japanese) with the occupation forces. Following the war, Geoff was in even greater demand. He worked with Australia's largest Tent Show, Barton's Follies and the Tivoli circuit and enjoyed trips that included Japan, England and Germany.

At this point, I ask Geoff about his nickname of Tangle-Tongue. Apparently it started as TangleFoot and when he was in charge of the concert party it was known as the TangleFoot Show. Later, at an audition for the Tivoli, Mori

Diamond who had the dancing school at the Tivoli, suggested he change the name to TangleTongue as it was not his foot he was tangling!

After a mug of coffee Geoff led me through to his lounge where he started to play a DVD which was a conversion of some of his 16mm film footage. The year was 1954 and Geoff was now married to Tabbi Frances and was stood alongside a 250cc motorcycle and sidecar outside his new brides parents London shop. It was the start of a journey – a journey from London to Sydney, Australia. The colour but soundless footage took me from one iconic location to another. A trip half way around the world from London to Sydney via Europe, Iraq, Iran, Pakistan, India (and the Taj Mahal) and Sri Lanka on a motorbike and side car that was clearly deteriorating as the journey progressed was documented. The film concluded with footage of the journey from Sri Lanka on a steamer to Fremantle and then the ride across the Nullarbor to Sydney arriving on boxing day. Amazing.

With such a background the foundations were starting to fall in place for Geoff to write a song about travelling everywhere. But there were still a few years to pass before the now iconic lyrics would be penned.

Geoff showed me some more 16mm footage with that familiar 1950's colourisation. In these following years Geoff and Tabby had teamed up with Lucky Grills to form the last of the big tent shows, Carol's Varieties. They bought the trucks and equipment and set out touring Australia for 10 months in every year performing song, dance and comedy to audiences across the country. The footage showed a number of acts performing with Geoff and Tabbi frequently on stage too.

Geoff said that, with the exception of him and Tabbi, all the other performers had now passed on.

And so we arrive in 1959 and Geoff had been working at a Holiday resort in Coolingatta in Queensland for some time when he received an invitation to perform a cabaret act in Sydney. He wanted to write an opening number for this new act so whilst sitting in his panel van, with maps for Queensland, New South Wales and Victoria alongside him, he started penning his opening act. Geoff confirmed that the song was written in Queensland, not Sydney as sometimes is reported and the maps available to him explain why, with the exception of Darwin, there are no towns in the song from the Northern Territory, West Australia, South Australia or Tasmania.

The original opening to the song (although Geoff will tell you its actually a chant) went "It's Nice to be back in Sydney and you ask me what I've seen, if you settle back and listen I'll tell you exactly where I've been" and took the title "The Swagman Rock" and soon became a mainstay of his act and became frequently requested.

In the mean time a music publisher from New Zealand, Johnny Devlon contacted Geoff seeking some songs that he would consider placing with his company. Geoff took along five of his best but Johnny had heard the song about the town names and wondered where that was – it was added to the collection of six songs after some modification to give it some proper verses.

In 1961 Geoff presented the his songs to the A&R manager at Festival Records in Sydney and was advised that he needed to change the name of "Swagman Rock" as rock and roll would be dead in a year. Geoff quickly changed the name himself to "I've been everywhere" as he had heard that using someone else's suggestion could result in a lower fee. I've been everywhere was officially born and in January 1962 I've been everywhere was recorded by Australian singer Lucky Starr. Surprisingly Geoff would not know of the initial success of his song until he heard it on the radio whilst working in Queensland. Thanks to the airtime it received it 'Everywhere' went straight to number one where it remained for fifteen weeks. Geoff thought he had a five minute wonder and continues to be surprised by its ongoing success.

At this point I hear the music coming from the kitchen as one of the versions of "I've been everywhere" continues to play. Geoff himself has written a number of versions including New Zealand, UK, USA and Canadian releases (all recorded by Lucky Starr as Lucky's Been Everywhere) and German and even Japanese versions as well as an edition using medical conditions instead of place names. As Geoff kindly cracks open a bottle of beer I ask him how he feels about being possibly best remembered for "I've been everywhere". He philosophically comments that you can not choose how you're remembered but did pass a comment about writer Bob Merrill who composed some amazing pieces but is best remembered as the novelty song "How much is that doggie in the window". Indeed, whilst the country music fraternity have adopted Geoff as one of their own and acknowledged his achievements with many awards, Geoff foremost considers himself an entertainer and variety artist.

Before heading off, I ask Geoff about several of the more difficult to locate locations in I've been everywhere and he thankfully helps solve a few puzzles for me. He also kindly signs a I've been everywhere record and some sheet music. We then walk out the lounge, past the closet containing the film and take a couple of photos by a wall containing some of his showbiz mementos, we say farewell, shake hands and depart.

As I wander down the footpath, I know that I've now just met the real "I've been everywhere" man and indeed, he has been to nearly all the locations in the song (he's not been to Birdsville yet) and many more besides. His film archive represents just a small glimpse into the full life he has lived. Thank you Geoff for sharing some time with me and for the opportunity to witness for myself what a great guy you are.

In memory of Albert Geoffrey McElhinney OAM (20 December 1922 – 21 July 2017).

The Geoff Mack Time Line

1922 Albert Geoffrey McElhinney was born on 20 December

1942 Geoff joined the RAAF as a mechanic but before long he was performing at concert parties.

1945 Whilst in Borneo Geoff is spotted by staff members of radio station 2SM whilst supporting Gracie Fields resulting in him doing some radio broadcasts and touring with Barton's Follies (Australia's largest Tent Show) followed on his return. Geoff then went to Japan with the occupation forces,

1947 Returns to Australia to work at the Tivoli before heading back to Japan.

1948 Geoff sails from Yokohama to England and then spends a year in Germany working for the American Special Services.

1950 Geoff returns to Sydney for 10 months working in clubs before going back to London to appear on BBC Television. Whilst visiting Germany met his wife to be, dancer and entertainer Tabbi Frances.

1954 The now married couple moved back to Australia but to put any future I've been anywhere into perspective drove on a motorbike all the way from London to Sydney via Europe, Iraq, Iran, Pakistan, India and Sri Lanka.

1962 January– Lucky Starr records I've been everywhere. It goes straight to number one in the Australian charts where it remains for 15 weeks.

1962 – Canadian Hank Snow recocrds I've been everywhere. It reaches number 1 in the US Country Music chart and 68 in the Billboard Hot 100 – the United States music industry standard singles popularity chart.

1963 Geoff was inducted into the International Songwriters Hall of Fame in Nashville, Tennessee

Mid 1960's Geoff meets Hank Snow who was touring Australia as part of Australian Country Music star Reg Lindsay's National tour.

1978 Inducted into the Hands of Fame, Tamworth NSW

1997 Tamworth Song Writer's Association Song Maker Award

2005 Medal of the Order of Australia for "service to country music and to the community, particularly through support for senior citizens' groups".

. . .

Must See

If you're passing through Tamworth — Australia's country music capital — check out Geoff Mack's plaque in the *Hands of Fame Park*. Tamworth also houses the Australian Country Music Hall of Fame, where Geoff's contribution is honoured alongside country music's greatest. You can also see the motorcycle he rode from the UK to Australia in 1954.

Fun Fact

Geoff Mack wasn't just a songwriter — he could sing "Old MacDonald Had a Farm" in Japanese! His love of languages and performance saw him entertain audiences around the world, from Japan to Germany, long before he became known as the "Everywhere Man."

Key Statistics

• Born: 20 December 1922, Surrey Hills, Victoria

• Wartime service: RAAF mechanic and concert party performer (1942–45)

• Legendary journey: Rode a motorbike and sidecar from London to Sydney via Europe, Iraq, Iran, Pakistan, India and Sri Lanka (1954)

• Wrote *I've Been Everywhere*: 1959 in Coolangatta, Queensland

- Awards: Inducted into Nashville's International Songwriters Hall of Fame (1963), *Hands of Fame* Tamworth (1978), Song Maker Award (1997)

- Medal of the Order of Australia: 2005 for service to country music and the community

THE JOURNEY

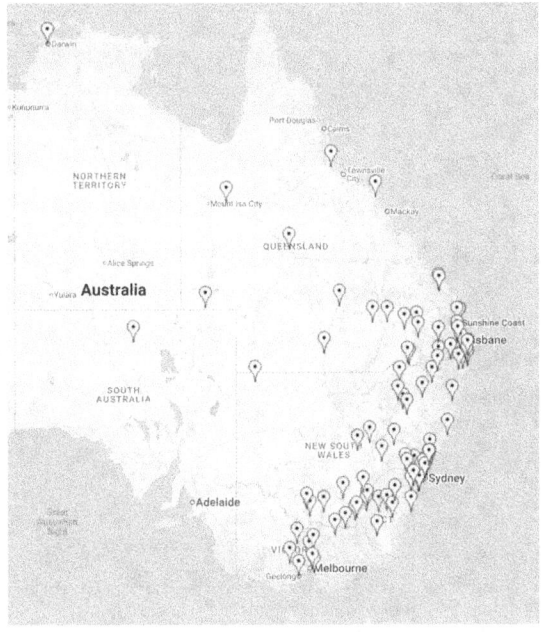

CHAPTER 1
TERRIGAL (NSW)

Of all the places in this wide brown land, my own home town of Terrigal happens to be one of the 93 locations immortalised in the classic *I've Been Everywhere* song. I reckon I've hit the jackpot. No long drive required — just my two feet and a short wander down the road.

Terrigal sits proudly on the New South Wales Central Coast — so named because it's smack-bang halfway between Sydney and Newcastle. In fact, if you're coming from either city it's an easy run: about an hour and a half by car or train (though technically you'll need to hop off at Gosford station, a short drive away).

The place was first settled by Europeans in 1826, but its name comes from the Aboriginal word "Tarragul", thought to mean *a place of little birds*. I chuckled at that when I thought about the massive pelicans that now cruise around like they own the joint.

During the week, Terrigal keeps things relaxed — a quiet, easygoing seaside town. But come Friday night or a sunny weekend, the place livens up as half of Sydney seems to descend for their coastal escape... while plenty of locals probably head the other way for a city fix!

The town centre hugs the waterfront, a modest stretch packed with real estate agencies, surf shops, a few banks and a chemist, along with a good mix of cafes, pubs and restaurants that'll suit most budgets. The Crowne Plaza looms large at the southern end of the beach — a local landmark that looks swanky enough, though it might just be popular because it's the only major hotel in town.

It's pretty easy to settle in here — take a stroll along the beach, grab a coffee, and soak up the salt air. But if you're up for a bit more action, a walk up *The Skillion* is an absolute must. This striking headland juts out dramatically and rewards anyone who makes the effort with breathtaking views back over the coastline. Words can't really do it justice — it's one of those places you just have to see.

And if you're after a classic beachside feed, there's a fish and chip shop nearby that's hands-down the friendliest and most reliable place in town for a serve of fresh, hot seafood.

Anyway, much as I love my hometown, this is where the journey really begins. Time to hit the road proper...

Fun Fact:

Despite being named for "little birds," Terrigal is best known for its pelicans, who gather in large numbers and look anything but small!

Must See:

- The Skillion lookout
- Terrigal Beach and Esplanade
- The Haven (great for a picnic or a paddle)

Key statistics:

- Population: approx. 12,000
- Located on the NSW Central Coast
- Main industries: tourism, hospitality, and small business

CHAPTER 2
KURRI KURRI (NSW)

It's a great feeling when a trip really *starts*, and for me that happened as I left Terrigal and headed north-west for Kurri Kurri, my second stop of the journey but the first real foray away from home. Departure was delayed slightly thanks to an itchy dog needing a trip to the vet (long story — ask me over a beer sometime), but finally, I was on my way.

Kurri Kurri is just 81 km from Terrigal — a short hop — but I couldn't resist visiting a town with a name like this. One of those quaint Aboriginal names that just sounds cheerful. Turns out "Kurri Kurri" actually means "Hurry Up!", which feels appropriate for the start of a road trip.

As I drove through the outskirts, I passed clusters of wooden houses and cottages before reaching the main shopping street, where I put my parking skills to the test — successfully slotting the car into a 45-degree parallel park with only a modest amount of faffing about (to the quiet amusement of the locals watching me from nearby benches).

First stop: the Tourist Information Centre. The friendly lady behind the counter, without hesitation, handed me leaflets and told me my mission: go find the murals and the newly constructed kookaburra. Simple enough.

As I wandered back down the main street, it dawned on me that I'd already seen some of these famous murals without even noticing them! They're everywhere: painted above shops, tucked into laneways, on side walls — bright, creative and varied in style, from cartoonish to classic realism. Since 2003, Kurri Kurri's artists have been busy, with the 50th mural unveiled just this year. And here's a fun detail — if you look closely, you'll spot a kookaburra hidden somewhere in every single mural.

After taking it all in, I set off to find the town's newest attraction — the Big Kookaburra in Memorial Park. Sure enough, there it was: a kookaburra about two metres tall, perched proudly on its concrete plinth behind a temporary work fence as local tradies put the finishing touches on it. The sculpture was cleverly aged so it looked like it had been there forever — a nice touch.

Whether it will earn a spot among Australia's long list of "Big Things" (Bananas, Apples, Mangos, Prawns — even, believe it or not, a Big Turd somewhere) remains to be seen. But it's certainly big enough to get my attention and worthy of a photo.

With my "must-see" list for Kurri Kurri ticked off, I returned to my car and discovered that getting out of a 45-degree parking space is much easier than getting in. A small victory to round out a pleasant little stop.

. . .

Fun Fact:

Since 2003, Kurri Kurri's murals project has made it the "Town of Murals", and spotting the hidden kookaburra in each mural has become a favourite challenge for visitors.

Must See:

- Kurri Kurri murals — vibrant and creative, with kookaburras hidden in every one
- Big Kookaburra — about two metres tall and destined to become a quirky landmark
- Main street — take a stroll and soak in the atmosphere of this tidy, friendly town

Key Statistics:

- Population: Approx. 6,000
- Location: Hunter Region, NSW
- Elevation: About 80 metres above sea level
- Known for: Murals, kookaburras (both real and artistic), friendly small-town feel

CHAPTER 3
GUNNEDAH (NSW)

After my morning visit to Kurri Kurri, it was time to hit the road again, heading for my next destination — Gunnedah. The route took me through the Hunter Valley, where the scenery is a curious mix of rolling countryside and coal mining activity. The mines themselves are discreetly tucked away from the road, but protest signs make sure you don't forget they're there.

As I neared Quirindi, the landscape changed noticeably. The land flattened out, framed by the distant Liverpool Ranges, and everything started looking just that little bit more outback. The grass had turned that familiar dry, burnt brown; everything was dusty; cattle clustered under lonely trees for shade; and the occasional windmill lazily creaked, waiting in vain for a breeze. The sky was classic Aussie blue — clear except for one lone cloud that looked like it might evaporate at any second.

Having turned off the New England Highway miles back, traffic eased and soon I had the road almost entirely to myself — apart from the cattle who seemed to think they owned it.

A few hundred head grazed peacefully at the roadside, occasionally wandering casually across the tarmac as if to remind me who was really in charge around here. It was all rather pleasant and felt like a nostalgic return to my childhood on the family farm.

After about four hours on the road, I rolled into Gunnedah and checked into my digs for the night — the Alyn Motel on Conadilly Street, the town's main drag. Before unpacking too much, I asked the locals for their "must see" recommendation. The answer was immediate: Koalas. Gunnedah proudly proclaims itself as the "Koala Capital of the World".

Apparently, I had two options:

1. Head up to Porcupine Lookout to spot them in the wild, or

2. Visit Waterways Wildlife Park to see them up close and personal.

Determined to see these iconic Aussie marsupials in their natural habitat, I chose the lookout.

Porcupine Lookout is well positioned to give a cracking view over the town and the surrounding plains. From up there, you really get a sense of just how flat this country is — with the Liverpool Ranges sitting hazily on the horizon. Unfortunately, I must report that my quest for a wild koala was unsuccessful. Not a furry ear or sleepy face in sight.

Given my earlier failure to spot murals in Kurri Kurri, perhaps I should have known better. Clearly, my wildlife-spotting skills leave a lot to be desired.

Still, the view was worth the climb. And after my unsuccessful koala hunt, I headed back into town to search for some food — thankfully a much more successful mission. I consoled myself over dinner by reminiscing about the times I *have* seen koalas... in captivity.

Fun Fact:

Gunnedah's claim as the "Koala Capital of the World" isn't just tourist hype — the surrounding countryside is ideal koala habitat, and wild populations thrive here thanks to abundant eucalypts and low levels of urbanisation.

Must See:

- Porcupine Lookout — even if the koalas are elusive, the view is superb
- Waterways Wildlife Park — for a guaranteed koala sighting
- Stroll along Conadilly Street — charming small-town atmosphere
- Gunnedah's local murals and sculptures celebrating its rural heritage

Key Statistics:

- Population: Approx. 9,000
- Location: North West Slopes, NSW
- Elevation: Around 264 metres
- Known for: Koalas, rural lifestyle, and links to poet Dorothea Mackellar ("My Country")

CHAPTER 4
NARRABRI (NSW)

After checking in at the Narrabri Tourist Information Office, I was told there were two "must-see" attractions in the area: the Sawn Rock formation and the CSIRO Australia Telescope.

Unfortunately, thanks to bushfires in the region, Sawn Rock was a no-go zone, so that left me with the telescope — and this turned out to be a hidden gem.

Australia really does know how to keep a secret. I'd heard of (and seen) the giant radio telescope at Parkes — made famous thanks to the film *The Dish* — but I hadn't realised there were five more equally impressive dishes tucked away about 20 km west of Narrabri.

These five 22-metre-wide dishes are mounted on railway tracks (yes, actual tracks!) and can be seen pointing in different directions into the deep blue sky. Despite their individual appearance, they work together as though they are one really big telescope, cleverly combining signals to create sharp images of far-off cosmic objects.

And here's the odd part — while the guidebook assured me there should be six dishes, there were only five in view. Wandering around the eerily quiet visitor centre — alone, with not even a staff member in sight — I wondered if the sixth dish had simply wandered off! Later I discovered that the sixth dish is located about 3 km further west, away from the main array. Mystery solved.

After *"doing the dishes"* (sorry — couldn't resist that one), I headed back into Narrabri, a pleasant, practical country town and my base before continuing north on the journey.

Fun Fact:

Although less famous than Parkes, the Narrabri Telescope Array is just as important — it's one of Australia's key radio astronomy sites and is operated by the CSIRO as part of Australia's cutting-edge science infrastructure.

Must See:

- Australia Telescope Compact Array — five massive dishes (plus a sixth hidden one) all working as a giant radio telescope
- Narrabri town centre — classic regional NSW town atmosphere
- If open: Sawn Rock, a striking natural rock formation just outside town

Key Statistics:

- Population: Approx. 6,000

- Location: North West Slopes, NSW
- Elevation: About 212 metres
- Known for: Astronomy, agriculture (cotton and wheat), Sawn Rock formation

CHAPTER 5
MOREE (NSW)

Today, the radio announcer declared it was "weather for golliwogs". Now, that's not an expression I'd heard before — and honestly, I wasn't quite sure what he was on about. Thankfully, he quickly explained: it's weather that's neither too hot nor too cold. Perfect, in other words. And he was right — it really was a pearler of a day.

I rolled into Moree under clear skies and a pleasant 25 degrees. As usual, I made a beeline for the local tourist information office and posed my standard question: *"What's the must-see around here?"* The friendly lady behind the counter didn't hesitate. *"Have you got your swimming togs?"* she asked, eyes twinkling. When I nodded, she launched into an enthusiastic recommendation for the Moree Mineral Baths.

Togs and towel in hand, I wandered just a couple of blocks to the famous baths. Moree's thermal pools have a serious reputation — apparently, they're legendary for their healing powers. So much so that around 300,000 people make the pilgrimage here every year. (And don't worry — despite that volume, the water was beautifully clear.)

I was grateful to discover a whole array of pools, especially as a coachload of boisterous five-year-olds had just arrived for their swimming lesson. Fortunately, the littlies stuck to their own pool, leaving me to sample the two large hot pools. One was a toasty 38 degrees, while the other clocked in at a proper 40.5 — and let me tell you, that 2.5-degree difference felt *huge*. There's also a full-size Olympic pool (unheated), a junior pool, and a toddlers' pool. I stayed loyal to the hot ones, thank you very much.

The water itself comes straight from bores sunk deep into the Great Artesian Basin — an ancient underground water source that stretches beneath much of inland Australia. As for those healing powers? Well, I'll keep you posted on that front. But floating there in the warm water on a perfect day, it sure felt good for the soul.

Fun Fact

Moree sits right on the Great Artesian Basin — one of the largest underground freshwater reservoirs in the world, covering about a fifth of Australia!

Must See

- Moree Artesian Aquatic Centre: Home of the famous mineral baths — relax in the hot pools and let the warm artesian waters work their magic.
- Moree Heritage Walk: A self-guided walk around some of Moree's handsome historic buildings.
- Bank Art Museum Moree (BAMM): A small but excellent regional art gallery housed in an old bank.

Key statistics

- Population: Around 8,000
- Location: Northern New South Wales, about 640 km from Sydney
- Claim to fame: Renowned for its artesian mineral baths and as a major agricultural centre, particularly for cotton.

CHAPTER 6
BOGGABILLA (NSW)

Boggabilla's a classic small town — blink and you'll miss it — but that's what makes it feel like a proper road-trip stop. It's very much a "one horse town" kind of place. One shop, one post office (closed when I passed through), one hotel (the Wobbly Boot) and one church.

Even the name, *Boggabilla*, has a simple honesty to it — meaning "full of creeks" in the local Aboriginal language.

It's the sort of place where you drive through, take a moment to appreciate the quiet, and perhaps pause to wonder about all the creeks that gave the town its name. Then, back on the road you go.

Fun Fact:

The name *Boggabilla* comes from the Gamilaraay language, roughly translating to "full of creeks" — very fitting for this quiet riverside settlement near the NSW-Queensland border.

Must See:

- The sign as you enter town
- The shop, church and post office (just so you can say you've ticked them off)

Key statistics:

- Population: approx. 529. 58 % of residents identify as Indigenous being part of the Kamilaroi tribe of the Plains.
- Location: near the NSW-Queensland border, just south of Goondiwindi
- Known for: being small, quiet, and… full of creeks!

CHAPTER 7
GOONDIWINDI (QLD)

Goondiwindi — sitting just over the New South Wales border in Queensland — has long been a town defined by its position. In years gone by, a *Customs House* was built here to collect taxes on goods crossing between states, a reminder of the time when Queensland and New South Wales felt just a little more separate.

It's also where I officially switch to Queensland time — one hour behind New South Wales at the moment, just to keep things interesting for travellers like me.

There's something unmistakable about a Queensland country town, though it's hard to pin down exactly what it is. A bit more warmth in the sun, a distinctive blend of old and new buildings, and those extra-friendly Queenslanders who all greet you with a "How ya going?" as you wander down the high street. It's like crossing that border brings you into a slightly different Australia — sunnier, slower, and a bit more laid-back.

The *Tourist Information Office* was my first port of call, where I quickly made a new friend — the assistant, a delightful 79-year-old lady who told me she'd just celebrated her birthday last month and happened to be the wife of a former mayor. When I asked what Goondiwindi's "must-see" attraction was, she smiled cheekily and declared, "Me!"

I assured her it was indeed a pleasure to meet her, but pressed for a second recommendation — this time she sent me across the road to the *Customs House Museum*.

At the museum I was greeted by a barefoot middle-aged woman (she apologised immediately for not having her shoes on — classic country hospitality!) and for just $3, I was taken on a guided tour. The museum itself is a quirky little treasure trove of local history: photographs, artefacts and tales of the town's major floods.

Whether these floods led to the creation of Goondiwindi's *Water Park* is unclear, but I learned that the park was once used for water skiing, boating and swimming... until, somewhat awkwardly, the water seeped out through the bottom and never really returned!

As for the name: *Goondiwindi* means "resting place of the birds" — and for this weary traveller, it felt like my resting place too, at least for the night.

Fun Fact:

Goondiwindi's name comes from an Aboriginal word meaning "resting place of the birds"

Must See:

- Customs House Museum — a slice of Goondiwindi history
- The Victoria Hotel — a classic country pub
- The "Elephant Tree" — a striking local landmark

Key statistics:

- Population: approx. 6,300
- Location: Southern Queensland, just north of the NSW border on the Macintyre River
- Known for: customs history, warm Queensland hospitality, and being a border town with character

CHAPTER 8
CUNNAMULLA (QLD)

This day was a big one — only one *"I've Been Everywhere"* town ticked off, but what a journey to get there. I set off from Goondiwindi, through St George, before finally pulling into Cunnamulla, well and truly feeling that I was venturing deep into the outback.

With every kilometre clocked, the trappings of civilisation thinned out — replaced by red dirt, gum trees and that endless ribbon of bitumen stretching ahead. St George itself was a pleasant stop. The Queensland hospitality was in full swing: I wandered into the Westpac branch and was greeted as though I was royalty — or maybe just their first visitor in months (probably the latter, to be fair).

After St George, I pulled into Bollon — although calling it a *town* would be generous; *"place"* felt more accurate. Bollon's claim to fame, it turns out, is sheep shearing. Debbie, behind the counter at the tiny store, proudly informed me that her husband once held a world record for sheep shearing — although, amusingly, the shearers apparently travel up to 600km these days just to find a sheep to shear.

Lunch at Debbie's was basic but hearty — meat pies served with condiments presented in oil cans. I loved that: classic outback improvisation.

Not long after leaving Bollon, the wildlife parade began. First, I spotted my very first emu in the wild, striding through the scrub with a chick in tow. A few kilometres later, an entire emu family crossed the road right in front of me. Then it was wild goats... then kangaroos bounding across my path. The outback was putting on a show, and I was loving it.

But the road had other plans. Somewhere between St George and Cunnamulla, just after bouncing over a cattle grid, I heard a suspicious bang. A few minutes later, the tyre warning light glowed helpfully on the dash. I pulled over, hoping it was just a dodgy sensor, but no such luck — a loud hiss confirmed I was going nowhere fast.

In typical optimistic fashion, I briefly went into denial mode and turned off the radio, just in case the hissing was coming from that instead (as if!). No luck. The tyre was deflating before my very eyes.

So there I was — changing a tyre in 40-degree heat, cursing my earlier smugness about being "prepared" (I'd stocked up on bananas and water thinking this would *guarantee* a smooth run — turns out life doesn't work that way).

Eventually, I rolled into Cunnamulla and got the tyre patched up for a bargain $25. Can't complain about that.

Cunnamulla itself — name meaning "long stretch of water" — felt like a town that had seen better days. The wide high street hinted at past prosperity, but now things looked a bit worn around the edges. I made my way to the Visitor Information Centre, where I was told the two *must-sees* were:

1 The bronze statue of the Cunnamulla Fella, erected in 2004 as a tribute to the Slim Dusty song, and

2 The historic Post Office, dating back to 1890 and built on the site of an old Cobb & Co stockyard.

Inside the tourist shop, I asked for a postcard and a bottle of water, and in true small-town fashion, the helpful shopkeeper cheerily walked me three doors down to her grocery store to grab one — talk about personal service.

But honestly, the most impressive sight of all wasn't man-made. At around 7pm, I drove just out of town and watched a fiery red sun melt into the red dirt and scrubby trees — a classic outback sunset, beautiful and utterly priceless.

Fun Fact:

The Cunnamulla Fella statue immortalises a character from Slim Dusty's famous song, and the town proudly leans into this bush legend.

Must See:

- The Cunnamulla Fella statue
- Cunnamulla Post Office (1890)
- Bollon: Debbie's cafe and sheep shearing stories
- Outback sunset viewing just outside town

Key statistics:

- Population: Approx. 1,200
- Distance: 489 km from Goondiwindi (via St George)

- Name meaning: "Long stretch of water" (Aboriginal origin)

CHAPTER 9
AUGATHELLA (QLD)

My day began in Cunnamulla and ended in Augathella, with 284 kilometres of classic outback driving in between — endless horizons and the occasional roo carcass to break the monotony.

First stop was *Wyandra*, a tiny village that proudly declared itself *Tidy Village 2002* (a title that still felt relevant). The Wyandra Post Office and Stores beckoned with a sign promising "Friendly Service" — and it wasn't false advertising. Kim and her husband greeted me warmly, serving up a great pot of coffee and a friendly chat.

They'd moved here around 2007 when the place apparently looked like a lunar landscape — today it was surprisingly green, thanks to small, steady downpours. The store's water comes straight from a bore sunk into the Great Artesian Basin back in 1910 — piping hot at 45°C straight from the earth and supplying both water and heating for the house.

Having had a shower that very morning in artesian water at Cunnamulla, I could vouch for its... shall we say, *distinctive* sulphur smell. I did wonder whether I smelled better or worse afterwards, but the water is beautifully soft — a drop of soap foams up like nobody's business.

After buying a couple of souvenir Wyandra mugs (how could I resist?) it was time to move on.

Next stop: *Charleville*. The town boasts the *Cosmos Centre*, making it a perfect destination for stargazers — but maybe better visited at night. My visit was short, just long enough for a rather unusual encounter in a public toilet where a frog sat in the bowl, staring up at me before making a swift escape down the U-bend. When I told the assistant at the Cosmos Centre, she looked at me like I was rarer than some of their meteorites.

Charleville also served up another surprise: a distinctive outback stench wafting through the hardware aisle of the local IGA. It was remarkably similar to the pong you get from decaying roo carcasses along the highway. I couldn't quite pinpoint the source — maybe a rogue roo, maybe a particularly ripe workman. Either way, it didn't seem to bother the locals, who were happily getting on with their shopping.

By early afternoon I finally rolled into *Augathella* — goal reached. The town was so quiet it felt almost like a film set for an outback ghost town, everything closed for the Saturday arvo. But it was a neat, tidy little place — well-spaced shops, all freshly painted — and clearly a community that took pride in their town, even if they were all elsewhere when I arrived.

Not keen to linger alone, I carried on to *Blackall* via Tambo to stay the night. Blackall is about the same size as Cunnamulla (around 1,160 people) but felt completely different — prosperous, well-maintained, and with a certain confidence about it, even if everything was shut.

Blackall has some cracking claims to fame. Legendary shearer *Jack Howe* set a world record here in 1892, shearing 321 sheep in 7 hours and 40 minutes — a record for hand shears that still stands today, only beaten with electric shears in 1950.

Then there's *The Black Stump*. Blackall lays claim to one of the "original" Black Stumps — that mythical marker denoting where the "outback" really begins. Of course, several other towns claim the same honour, so who knows which one's right? But Blackall's got a good stump and a good story, so I'm happy to let them have it.

And just outside town, there's a stretch of the famous *Dog Fence* — the wild dog barrier that once stretched 5,600 km across Australia and today still stands at about 2,500 km long, protecting vast tracts of grazing land from marauding dingoes.

Fun Fact:

Jack Howe's shearing record — 321 sheep in 7 hours and 40 minutes using hand shears — remains unbeaten by hand shearers today.

Must See:

- Wyandra Post Office and Stores — genuine outback hospitality
- Charleville Cosmos Centre (best after dark!)
- Augathella's quiet, tidy streets

- Blackall's Jack Howe monument
- The Black Stump (wherever it really is!)
- Dog Fence — Australia's longest fence and a true outback icon

Key statistics:

- Wyandra population: approx. 100
- Charleville population: approx. 3,000
- Augathella population: approx. 400
- Blackall population: approx. 1,160
- Location: All these towns sit along Queensland's Matilda Way, a classic outback driving route.

CHAPTER 10
MORELLA (QLD)

Today's journey started in *Blackall* and ended 393 km later in *Winton*, taking in *Longreach* and the only "I've Been Everywhere" town along the way — *Morella*.

I feel like I'm really starting to get the hang of this outback motoring business. I've adopted the laid-back stance, and I'm nearly perfecting that casual outback finger wave to oncoming drivers (when I say finger, I mean first finger — all very polite). True outback fashion probably calls for one elbow — or maybe a whole arm — dangling out the window, but I'm too attached to my air-conditioning for that.

By now I'm used to dodging dead kangaroos, weaving around road trains and breaking up the journey with plenty of stops. The scenery never feels monotonous — although, I admit, the only radio station broadcasting cricket all day did test that theory today.

Before leaving Blackall, I couldn't resist visiting the statue of *Jack Howe* — the legendary shearer who managed to hand-shear 321 sheep in 7 hours and 40 minutes, a record that still stands.

From there it was on to *Longreach*, a town I've long wanted to visit. And it didn't disappoint.

Longreach isn't one of the 93 towns in the song, but I indulged myself with a stop here — because two attractions were calling my name: the *QANTAS Founders Museum* and the *Australian Stockman's Hall of Fame*.

Rural Australian museums can often be charmingly simple — but not these two. They're world-class and wouldn't look out of place in Canberra or any global capital.

At the QANTAS Founders Museum, my aviation nerdiness was well catered for — with fascinating displays, artefacts and audiovisuals tracing the pioneering days of Australian flight. The highlight? Being able to climb aboard two historic aircraft: a *747-200* and a beautifully restored *Boeing 707*, VH-XBA — Australia's first passenger jet. With panels removed from the jumbo jet, I got to see its inner workings — but the classic 707 stole the show for me.

Then it was on to the *Stockman's Hall of Fame* — a tribute to Australia's unsung outback heroes. The museum is packed with stories of exploration, farming, and resilience, beautifully curated and well worth a visit.

But as much as I enjoyed Longreach, it was time to press on — because it's not in the lyrics! So at around 2pm, I drove the final 90 km west to *Morella*.

Now, *Morella* is small. Really small. The only thing I could find marking Morella's existence was the *Queensland Country*

Women's Association Morella Branch shed. That's it. I believe the "district" surrounds this shed, probably consisting of scattered homesteads.

Even so — Morella makes the list. Another town ticked off, even if it was nothing more than a name, a shed, and a spot to pause before continuing.

With the temperature nudging into the low 40s, I didn't linger long. I headed straight to *Winton*, where I found accommodation and settled in to write this update.

Tomorrow, it's time for a little detour: *Boulia* and the mysterious *Min Min lights*. It's not on the "I've Been Everywhere" list... but honestly, I can't resist this one. I'm genuinely excited about it — stay tuned!

Fun Fact:

Jack Howe's legendary 321-sheep hand-shearing record, set in 1892, still stands today and was only surpassed with the introduction of machine shears.

Must See:

- Jack Howe statue, Blackall
- QANTAS Founders Museum, Longreach
- Australian Stockman's Hall of Fame, Longreach
- Queensland Country Women's Association shed, Morella (about all there is!)

Key statistics:

- Morella population: almost nil
- Location: 90 km west of Longreach, Queensland
- Known for: being a district with a shed... and a place name in *I've Been Everywhere*.

CHAPTER 11
CLONCURRY (QLD)

Boulia (QLD)

Now, I have to admit straight up — Boulia isn't actually in the *I've Been Everywhere Man* song. But come on, how could I not take a detour out here? This is Min Min light country, after all.

I left Winton bright and early, setting my sights on Boulia some 300 kilometres away. Normally, that's a nice three-hour jaunt at 100–110km/h — enough to roll in just in time for lunch. But oddly, my GPS reckoned I wouldn't get there until 3:45pm. Same distance, same destination... very different arrival time. I should have known then that this wasn't going to be your average drive.

About halfway, I pulled into Middleton for a much-needed coffee. Val and her husband were behind the counter and pointed me towards the old Min Min Hotel site, about 80km outside Boulia. And like any curious traveller, I couldn't resist.

The Min Min Hotel itself is long gone — it burnt down in 1917, around the same time those mysterious Min Min lights first started appearing in this area. But the spot still has stories to tell. I found the dirt track leading off the main road, drove in about 500 metres, and there it was: a lonely sign marking the site's history, scattered shards of old glass glinting in the sun, and, most eerily of all, a single grave out the back.

Legend has it that the Min Min Hotel was no five-star retreat — it was more a rough-and-tumble joint where theft, murder, and prostitution were par for the course. So who knows how many souls might be buried out there? The place gave me the chills, and before long I decided to scarper — movies like *Wolf Creek* will do that to you!

Back on the road, I was soon confronted by something else entirely: splat... splat splat... ping! A storm of locusts battering the windscreen and radiator. Not quite a biblical plague, but enough to give the nerves a jolt.

As I closed in on Boulia, the roadkill seemed to ramp up too — dead kangaroos (no surprises there), then dead dingoes, a few flattened lizards for variety, and finally, just for good measure, a half-rotted cow. By the time I reached Boulia's welcome sign I was well and truly ready for coffee... and a stiff drink wouldn't have gone astray either.

But Boulia did not disappoint. I made straight for the Min Min Encounter Exhibition. At first, panic struck — I'd missed the last show of the day! But the lovely lass behind the counter took pity on me and fired up a private showing. The whole experience kicked off in a pitch-dark room with a talking dummy and proceeded from there. I won't spoil the details — it's 45 minutes of quirky, eerie entertainment that you really have to see for yourself.

After that I wandered town a bit: shot some video for friends, admired the town's enormous windmill, snapped a photo of the iconic Red Stump marking the Outback boundary, and visited the Stone House Museum with its impressive dinosaur fossil collection.

By the end of the day, it was motel check-in time — and I was ready to collapse. Between locusts, dingoes, graves and ghost lights, Boulia had well and truly got under my skin.

Fun Fact:

The origin of the name "Min Min" is still debated — no one really knows whether the lights were named after the old Min Min Hotel, or if the hotel took its name from the lights!

Must See:

- Min Min Encounter Exhibition: A one-of-a-kind audio-visual show telling the tales of the mysterious Min Min lights.
- The Red Stump: Symbolically marking the start of the Outback.
- Stone House Museum: For a peek at pioneer history and local dinosaur fossils.
- The big windmill: Boulia's landmark windmill — an obligatory photo stop.

Key Statistics:

- Location: Outback Queensland, around 300km southwest of Winton.
- Population: Approximately 300 hardy souls.
- Claim to fame: Min Min lights — eerie, unexplained lights reported in the area for over a century.

Cloncurry (QLD)

This report is a short one — for three good reasons. Firstly, after driving over 1,100 km today, I'm completely bushed. Secondly, most of that driving was through classic outback country: long, straight, shimmering-hot roads where not much happened (other than spotting the occasional cow stubbornly parked in the middle of the bitumen). And thirdly... well, I've got Christmas cards to write!

So, on to Cloncurry.

I set off from Boulia this morning, headed north for Mount Isa, then turned east toward Cloncurry. I was genuinely looking forward to visiting *Cloncurry's Flying Doctor Museum*, as Cloncurry is proudly known as the birthplace of the Royal Flying Doctor Service. The very first flight of this legendary Aussie service took off from here on 15 May 1928.

But alas — on arrival I was greeted by a locked gate and a sign declaring the museum closed through December and January. Looks like I'll have to "pop back" in February... whenever that may be.

The weather was certainly doing its best to remind me of Cloncurry's record-breaking past. The mercury today hovered around 42°C — a solid effort, though still shy of the famous record set here in 1889 when the temperature reportedly hit 53.1°C.

That record, by the way, comes with a bit of a caveat: apparently, the temperature was measured in an improvised screen made from a beer crate, and later analysis suggests it was more like 47–49°C. Still hot enough to melt your thong plugs!

In the end, Cloncurry didn't quite live up to expectations — though in fairness, it was probably just too hot for anything much to happen. And besides, when the Flying Doctor Museum is shut, it leaves little else to do but tip your hat to the heat, find an air-conditioned spot, and move on.

Fun Fact:

Cloncurry is widely recognised as the birthplace of the Royal Flying Doctor Service — one of the world's most innovative and iconic aeromedical organisations.

Must See:

- The Flying Doctor Museum
- Cloncurry town centre — classic outback character
- Cloncurry's "heat history" and record-breaking temperatures

Key statistics:

- Population: approx. 2,700
- Location: northwest Queensland, between Mount Isa and Julia Creek
- Known for: searing heat, birthplace of the RFDS, rich outback history

CHAPTER 12
BAMBAROO (QLD)

Bambaroo is one of those blink-and-you'll-miss-it places — a district in North East Queensland about three hours south of Cairns, with not much more at its centre than a school. There's not a lot to report: no pub, no post office, no bustling main street... but it still earns its place in the lyrics of *I've Been Everywhere*, and that's good enough for me.

It also happens to be the most northerly of the Queensland locations on my journey — but that didn't stop me from pushing just a little further north to Cairns.

Nine years ago — almost to the day — I first set foot on Australian soil right here in Cairns, so I couldn't resist a bit of a nostalgic detour. It was a chance to revisit my Australian beginnings.

And honestly, Cairns hasn't changed much. It's still that bustling, multicultural, backpacker-filled holiday town. My old backpackers is still standing, and so are the pizza and kebab stalls lining the esplanade, doing a roaring trade with the international crowd. The humidity? As oppressive as ever

— like walking into a sauna the moment you step outdoors. And the pushy restaurant staff are still there too, hustling for business and trying to lure passing tourists into their establishments with special offers and persuasive smiles.

Cairns feels almost theatrical — a bit of an Aussie stage show created to match the tourist dream of Australia: palm trees, crocs, reefs, and all the clichés served up together.

Having just come from the outback, I couldn't help but notice the contrast. *Tourist Cairns* is fun, friendly, and lively… but it's a show. A theme park version of Australia designed for visitors, rather than the real deal I'd just driven through.

That said, it's still a fun place to visit — and for me, it'll always be the place where my Australian journey began.

Fun Fact:

Bambaroo's name is believed to derive from an Aboriginal word meaning *"pool of water"* — fitting for a quiet district in wet tropical Queensland.

Must See:

- The school at Bambaroo (it's about the only landmark!)

Key statistics:

- Bambaroo population: fewer than 100
- Location: Far North Queensland
- Known for: Bambaroo — not much but it's on the song list

CHAPTER 13
PROSERPINE (QLD)

After 10 days on the road, I finally started heading south towards home... although with *2,300 km still to go*, "heading home" might be a bit optimistic!

Today's journey took me from a soggy *Cairns* down to *Proserpine*, just over 600 km away — a fitting journey given that today Queensland celebrated its 150th birthday. Yes, it's been 150 years since *Queen Victoria* granted Queensland statehood, separating it from New South Wales.

The drive today was a sharp contrast to my earlier outback travels. Where the outback offered endless ochre plains, dusty roads and maybe five other cars over 400 km, this stretch of the eastern seaboard offered a sea of *lush green*, thanks to generous rainfall, and a steady stream of traffic — more like 400 cars every five kilometres.

I much prefer outback motoring.

I stopped for breakfast at *Cardwell*, sitting by the pier with a coffee and enjoying the views (despite the grey weather), before pushing onwards.

By about 4:30pm I rolled into *Proserpine* and checked into a local motel. Proserpine itself is a pleasant enough town — but let's be honest, it's a gateway town. The sort of place that serves a purpose: it's the gateway to *Airlie Beach*, which itself is the gateway to the *Whitsundays*.

Proserpine is a little inland so it lacks that coastal holiday feel — but it's practical, with a decent shopping strip where you can get essentials (I stocked up on biscuits), a few motels and a couple of garages.

One thing worth noting: *Proserpine* isn't far from *Bowen*, home of the famous *Big Mango* — and if you fancy a mango, this is the place to go.

Fun Fact:

Proserpine is considered the "gateway to the Whitsundays" — but the town itself is inland, surrounded by cane fields and mango farms.

Must See:

- The Big Mango at Bowen (a short drive north)
- Proserpine's main street — handy for supplies
- Cardwell pier (if you're passing through en route)

Key statistics:

- Population: approx. 3,500
- Location: North Queensland, 20 km inland from Airlie Beach
- Known for: sugar cane, proximity to Airlie Beach and Whitsundays, and the nearby Big Mango

CHAPTER 14
GIN GIN (QLD)

Today I left *Rockhampton* — or *Rocky*, as the locals affectionately call it — and headed south to another Queensland destination: *Gin Gin*.

Gin Gin struck me as a genuinely thriving little town — full of activity, with locals and visitors alike going about their business. It felt busy, friendly, and alive — perhaps living up to its accolade as the holder of the *Friendliest Town Award*(2003).

The staff at the café where I stopped for a coffee and apple slice certainly did their part to uphold that title — warm smiles and genuinely helpful service. It's a simple pleasure but one that makes a difference on the road.

The other thing that caught my eye? The road markings — absolutely immaculate. I don't know if the linesman here is just especially proud of his work, but every street, crossing and kerb was sharply painted and looking spot-on.

Gin Gin: friendly folk, good coffee... and some of the sharpest white lines you'll ever see!

Fun Fact:

Gin Gin proudly won the *Friendliest Town Award* in 2003 — and judging by the café service, they're still living up to it!

Must See:

- Main street for a wander among friendly locals
- A coffee and apple slice at one of the cafés
- Immaculate white road markings (honestly, worth admiring)

Key statistics:

- Population: approx. 1,200
- Location: Bundaberg region, Queensland
- Known for: Friendly locals, crisp white road lines, and as a popular stop on the Bruce Highway

CHAPTER 15
WALLAVILLE (QLD)

Wallaville sits just down the road from Gin Gin — about a 15-minute drive — but it feels a world away when it comes to passing traffic. Most tourists zoom right by these days, thanks to the highway now skirting around this little village.

And that's exactly how Wallaville comes across: quiet, almost forgotten, as if it's gently dozing while the world rushes past. There's not much to detain you — a handful of houses, a sleepy main street, and that typical small-town charm.

But that's the beauty of a place like Wallaville: it doesn't try to impress or attract; it simply is. A genuine little Queensland village content in its own skin — and a nice reminder that sometimes the places just off the highway can offer the most peaceful pause.

Fun Fact:

Wallaville was historically part of the sugarcane industry that shaped this region and had its own sugar mill until it closed in 1978.

Must See:

- Take a slow drive through the village — blink and you might miss it
- Soak up the quiet rural atmosphere

Key statistics:

- Population: approx. 400
- Location: 15 minutes from Gin Gin, Queensland
- Known for: rural charm, sugarcane history, bypassed by the Bruce Highway

CHAPTER 16
KUMBARILLA (QLD)

After leaving Wallaville, I had quite a long stretch before reaching another *I've Been Everywhere* location. The road took me inland — not too far from the coast, but the scenery could be summed up in just two words: *gum trees*.

But as I pushed further inland, things began to feel more outback and, to my mind, far more appealing. The traffic thinned out too — the first day of the Christmas school holidays usually means caravans galore, but they were thankfully few and far between. What did puzzle me was the number of cars towing boats through this dry and dusty part of Queensland... maybe they were optimists?

As I neared Dalby, the skies opened and the rain poured down. So I decided to stop there for the night rather than soldier on in the deluge. But after the rain eased a little, I jumped back in the car and drove the final 40 km to *Kumbarilla*.

And what did I find at Kumbarilla? Not much, really.

A railway line. Two signs — one on either side of the track — both declaring *Kumbarilla*.

That was it. No pub, no shop, no bakery offering a meat pie... just a name on a map and a pair of signs to prove it exists.

Still, it's on the list — so it counts!

Fun Fact:

The name *Kumbarilla* is believed to come from an Aboriginal word, but records differ as to its exact meaning — possibly "broad-leaved ironbark" or "camp near water," even though there's not much water to be found here.

Must See:

- The railway track
- The two Kumbarilla signs (take a photo — that's about all you can do!)

Key statistics:

- Population: 223
- Location: about 40 km west of Dalby, Queensland
- Known for: Being subject to a petroleum lease for coal seam gas with a grid of wells and pipelines in the northern and south-western parts of the locality

CHAPTER 17
BRIGALOW (QLD)

After rain forced an unexpected overnight stay in Dalby (not that I minded — the motel was brand new and smelled faintly of fresh paint and ambition), I was up early and determined to tick off a few more of the non-coastal Queensland towns from the "I've Been Everywhere" song.

The route required a bit of weaving about — the kind of back-road zig-zagging that Queensland seems to specialise in — but first stop was Brigalow, a classic Darling Downs farming town. The population here hovers somewhere around 450 or so, though it felt like even fewer when I arrived: not a soul in sight, but plenty of tractors to keep me company.

Brigalow's claim to fame, at least visually, is its massive grain store, which looms over the highway like a rural skyscraper. Clearly this is a town where grain is king — wheat, barley, and probably a bit of sorghum thrown in for good measure.

On the way through I noticed a little brown sign pointing off to an "Historic Cemetery." Curious (and always partial to a quirky detour), I turned right as instructed, only to be met with that classic country Queensland experience: no further signage. No arrows, no explanations, nothing. Just me, the open paddocks, and an increasing suspicion that the cemetery had either vanished or was so historic it had returned to the earth.

In the end, the historic cemetery remains a mystery — at least to me. Perhaps next time I'll bring a local guide, or at least someone with better navigation skills than mine.

Fun Fact:

Brigalow gets its name from the native Brigalow tree (*Acacia harpophylla*), once widespread across the Downs but now cleared for agriculture.

Must See:

- That enormous grain silo — you really can't miss it.
- For adventurous souls: the elusive historic cemetery (good luck).

Key Statistics:

- Location: Darling Downs, Queensland
- Population: Approx. 181
- Known for: Agriculture, especially grain production

CHAPTER 18
CONDAMINE (QLD)

Today a detour took me 33 kilometres off the main drag to reach this tiny town called Condamine. It's the sort of place that, on first glance, looks a lot like Brigalow — classic small-town Queensland, with wide streets, modest buildings, and a distinct air of unhurried country life.

The drive here gave me a peek at Chinchilla, too — home of the famous Melon Festival. I didn't stop this time but made a mental note to return; I'm a bit intrigued by the thought of melon skiing and pip spitting contests!

Condamine's claim to fame is a humble but iconic bit of bush ingenuity: the Condamine Bell. This small bell, knocked together from sheet metal, was used by drovers to keep track of their cattle mobs as they grazed across vast properties. Handy bit of kit when your herd's spread over miles of bush! There's even a picture of the bell proudly displayed on the town sign as you roll in — a fitting nod to local history.

Pulling into the truck stop, I grabbed a hearty breakfast and took the chance to soak up some local yarns from the pinboard inside. Tales of past floods and even a rather subdued street parade from 1946 caught my eye — sounds like Condamine's seen its share of excitement, though you wouldn't guess it from the quiet streets today.

Fun Fact:

The Condamine Bell became so popular that versions of it were soon used across Australia by drovers and graziers — making Condamine a household name in cattle country.

Must See:

- The Condamine town sign with its image of the famous bell
- Truck stop café (perfect for a solid country brekkie)
- Take a drive through nearby Chinchilla — especially during Melon Festival time!

Key Statistics:

- Population: Around 150
- Location: 33 km off the Warrego Highway, Queensland
- Known for: Birthplace of the Condamine Bell

CHAPTER 19
WALLUMBILLA (QLD)

After rejoining the main *A2 highway*, I carried on until I reached *Wallumbilla*.

Strangely, the three towns I visited today all seem to share a similar look and feel — a kind of agricultural twin-set, if you will. I suppose it's no surprise really; the terrain and cropping in this part of Queensland shape these places into their familiar forms: grain silos on the horizon, a smattering of shops, a pub or two, and tidy houses spread out across a mostly flat landscape.

Even though Wallumbilla sits quite a distance from any major city, it's clear this isn't "bush" country. The landscape here is working land — productive farmland rather than rugged outback — and that gives it its own unique character.

There's a quiet industriousness about Wallumbilla: not much happening on the surface, but you just know the locals are hard at work keeping things ticking over.

The name Wallumbilla was the name of a pastoral run leased by Charles Coxen, The name is presumed to come from the indigenous Mandandanji language and reportedly means plenty of jew fish.

So, after a quick look around — and ticking another "I've Been Everywhere" town off the list — it was time to roll on again.

Fun Fact:

Wallumbilla sits in prime *cropping country* — wheat, sorghum and other grains dominate the fields around town, giving it that open, pastoral look so typical of this part of inland Queensland.

Must See:

- Wallumbilla's grain silos and rural main street
- Agricultural scenery along the A2 highway

Key statistics:

- Population: approx. 331
- Location: Western Downs region, Queensland
- Known for: grain farming, relaxed country-town atmosphere

CHAPTER 20
MUCKADILLA (QLD)

Muckadilla — what a name. Honestly, it's hard to say Muckadilla without smiling, and I reckon the locals know it too.

This little spot sits in grain country and, much like today's other towns, it has that familiar outback look: a grain store, a modest collection of buildings, and a pub that feels like the heart of the place.

But while there may not be a lot here, Muckadilla has personality — and a sense of humour. Right outside the pub, I spotted two seats thoughtfully labelled: one the "Seat of Knowledge", and the other the "Bench of Bullshit". I didn't sit long enough to decide which was which — but it gave me a chuckle and told me everything I needed to know about the spirit of the place.

There's not much else to report from here. The town is far too small for major attractions — although I did notice what looked like a surprisingly well-maintained Rifle Club. It was unattended when I visited, so sadly I wasn't able to find out more... or take a shot myself!

So, after a quick look around and a smile at those bench signs, it was time to head off again, leaving Muckadilla to its quiet business.

Fun Fact:

The name *Muckadilla* is thought to come from an Aboriginal word meaning "plenty of water" — ironic really, considering the dry, dusty feel of the place today.

Must See:

- Muckadilla Pub's "Seat of Knowledge" and "Bench of Bullshit" — worth a photo at least
- The Rifle Club (if you can find someone home!)
- Classic country town vibe

Key statistics:

- Population: approx. 331
- Location: Western Queensland, west of Roma on the Warrego Highway
- Known for: cheeky benches, tiny-town charm, and a great name that's hard to say without grinning

CHAPTER 21
BOUINDARRA / BUNDARRA (NSW)/ BOROONDARA (VIC) *

The journey south continued as I made my way home for a well-earned break over Christmas. After an overnight stop in *Moree*, I set off down the *New England Highway*, with one last diversion to tick off a mysterious entry from the *I've Been Everywhere* song: *Bouindarra*.

Now, *Bouindarra* is a curious one — no one seems able to locate it. Various online discussions suggest it might be a mishearing or a forgotten place, and for a while I wasn't sure where to point the bonnet. Two likely contenders emerged: *Bundarra*, a little town in northern NSW, and *Boroondara*, a district in Melbourne.

I decided on Bundarra first, for two reasons:

1 The spelling and pronunciation aren't too far off — just drop an 'o' and an 'i' and you're almost there.

2 Bundarra is charmingly remote, fitting nicely with the song's spirit of dusty backroads and out-of-the-way places.

Bundarra itself is a sleepy old town — quaint, quiet, and seemingly frozen in time. The name apparently means *grey kangaroo*, though none were hopping about during my visit. The high street is lined with lovely old buildings, most looking like they've stood unchanged since the 19th century, and they easily outnumbered the people.

One building in particular caught my eye: the local garage, built around 1890 and still in use today. A couple of locals were having a classic chin wag out the front as I strolled by — a scene straight out of an Aussie postcard.

After a friendly exchange with the assistant at the general store and a quick purchase of some provisions, I pressed on through the *Hunter Valley* (pausing to note how a few vineyards were calling my name) and eventually made it back to the Central Coast for a much-needed cuppa.

But that wasn't quite the end of this *Bouindarra* mystery...

UPDATE: Solving the *Bouindarra* mystery

A few months later, I had the pleasure of meeting *Geoff Mack*, the very man who wrote *I've Been Everywhere*. I couldn't resist asking him about *Bouindarra*.

His answer cleared it all up: Bouindarra wasn't a town at all — it was the name of a district in Melbourne, now known as the *City of Boroondara*, and, as it turns out, it was Geoff's own birthplace!

So, for the sake of completeness (and because no stone should be left unturned in this journey), I made a quick pilgrimage to *Boroondara*. I wandered the district of *Camber-

well, snapped a photo or two of the council offices, watched a few trams rumble by... and that was about it.

No dusty outback pub or local garage here — just a pleasant, leafy Melbourne suburb.

Fun Fact:

The name *Bundarra* comes from the Aboriginal word for *grey kangaroo*. As for *Bouindarra*, it turns out it's a lost district of Melbourne — Geoff Mack's hometown — now rebadged as *Boroondara*.

Must See (Bundarra):

- Bundarra's historic high street
- The old garage, still going strong after more than 130 years
- The sturdy bridge over the Gwydir River

Key statistics:

- Bundarra population: approx. 400
- Boroondara population: approx. 180,000
- Location: Bundarra — northern NSW; Boroondara — eastern suburbs of Melbourne
- Known for: Bundarra — old-world charm and a timeless garage; Boroondara — leafy streets and Melbourne's trams

CHAPTER 22
WYONG (NSW)

Three days at home and I was already getting itchy feet — this *I've Been Everywhere* project is addictive! I didn't go too far this time, though — just a quick local jaunt to Wyong, a round trip of about 60 km.

Wyong is practically on my doorstep, so no GPS required. But while it's close, it's not somewhere I visit often. Partly because anything you can get in Wyong you can usually find closer to home, and partly because getting there means driving the infamous Wyong Road. Don't get me wrong — it's a nice dual carriageway — but honestly, I reckon there are more roundabouts on that stretch than there are residents in the shire. By the time I arrived, I could still feel my head spinning from the endless circling!

I pulled into Wyong around 11 am to find the town centre bustling, with people busily going about their pre-Christmas shopping. Wyong itself is the administrative heart of Wyong Shire — lots of council offices, but the town centre wasn't really calling to me.

So I'd done a bit of homework and had two places on my hit list: first stop, the *Alison Homestead*.

Built around 1885 by Charles Alison, this charming old house is now home to the Wyong District Museum & Historical Society. Unfortunately, luck wasn't on my side — a big "Closed" sign hung on the door, and it wouldn't reopen until the new year. Still, it was worth a look from the outside. The homestead sits on two hectares of green lawns and colourful gardens, and even though I couldn't explore inside, I could imagine the historical treasures within — kerosene-powered toasters and irons, an Edison cylinder phonograph, dictographs, a 1922 washing machine, and old radios and telephones.

While I was taking a few photos, a couple of friendly horses wandered over to say hello — clearly curious about my presence.

Next stop was *Hakone*, a house built around 1912 by Albert Hamlyn Warner — a bit of an entrepreneurial character by all accounts. Before moving to Wyong, Albert had made his fortune laying water pipes in Elizabeth Street, Sydney, and investing in land around Burwood and Canley Vale. By 1903 he'd snapped up 12,000 acres in the Wyong Shire, built 13 shops in Wyong's main street (which still stand today), and over 100 private homes in the area. Quite the legacy for one bloke.

Sadly, my exploration ended at a big "Trespassers Will Be Prosecuted" sign out the front of Hakone (now called *Strathavon*), so I took the hint and decided to call it a day.

Fun Fact:

Wyong Road might just be the unofficial capital of round-abouts — a dizzying experience for drivers who like to keep count (or even those who don't).

Must See:

- Alison Homestead and gardens
- Wyong's historic main street, where many of Albert Warner's original shopfronts still stand
- The lovely countryside on the outskirts of town — watch out for curious horses

Key statistics:

- Population: approx. 4,300 (Wyong itself)
- Location: NSW Central Coast, about 90 km north of Sydney
- Known for: administrative centre of Wyong Shire, historic buildings, roundabouts!

CHAPTER 23
ETTALONG (NSW)

Ettalong is one of those places that's practically on my doorstep, yet I've only visited a handful of times over the years. It's tucked away on the New South Wales Central Coast — 'central' because it's halfway between Sydney and Newcastle — and it blends so seamlessly into Booker Bay, Umina and Blackwall that you could drive through and not realise you've changed suburbs.

The name Ettalong is of Aboriginal origin, meaning "drinking place" — fitting, though I doubt the original meaning referred to café brunches or lazy beers by the beach.

Despite a cloudy morning with rain threatening, I left Terrigal and pulled up at Ettalong Wharf about 25 minutes later. From here, you can catch a ferry over to Palm Beach — a nice option for a day out — though I learned that the much-hyped 'Fast Ferry' service to Sydney, promised to get you there in 40 minutes, won't be happening anytime soon... the ferry company having gone under before it ever really got going.

But I wasn't here for a ferry ride. I wandered towards the town centre, passing a few antique and bric-a-brac shops before finding myself at Ettalong Markets. These indoor markets are clearly *the* place to be on a Sunday morning. Locals and tourists alike were browsing through an eclectic mix of clothing, toys, jewellery, housewares, food and sweets. There was a definite pre-Christmas vibe, with plenty of shoppers on the hunt for bargains — so naturally, I joined in and picked up a few bits and pieces myself.

The town itself is modest — and so is the beach, which seemed more the domain of patient fishermen than surfers. Towering above it all is the Ettalong Beach Resort, the only building in town that really makes a dent in the skyline. It looked like it was doing a roaring trade, with plenty of people dining outdoors, thongs and sunnies as far as the eye could see.

There are quite a few eateries scattered around the town centre, and we settled on the Surf Sun Sand Café for brunch. Pleasantly surprised, I found the prices here far more reasonable than some of the trendier Central Coast and Sydney venues.

After brunch, suitably revived, it was time to head home. But as one clever local business slogan goes: *"Get along to Ettalong."* And you should — it's a perfect place for a lazy Sunday morning.

Fun Fact:

Ettalong's proximity to Palm Beach means you can literally take a ferry and arrive where they film *Home and Away* — Alf Stewart not guaranteed.

Must See:

- Ettalong Wharf — take in the view or catch a ferry to Palm Beach
- Ettalong Markets — vibrant, indoors and perfect for browsing
- Ettalong Beach — calm and uncrowded
- Local cafés — grab a coffee and soak up the relaxed vibe

Key Statistics:

- Population: Approx. 4,500
- Location: Central Coast, NSW
- Elevation: Around sea level
- Known for: Markets, ferry access to Palm Beach, small-town charm by the sea

CHAPTER 24
TUGGERAWONG (NSW)

Funny thing about Tuggerawong — it's right near home, but like so many places close by, I'd never bothered to visit. Turns out, it's a bit of a hidden gem. Small and sleepy by nature, this little suburb hugs the western shores of Tuggerah Lake — a broad coastal lagoon that also links up with Budgewoi Lake and Lake Munmorah further north.

Driving through Tuggerawong's main street, it didn't exactly scream "tourist hotspot" — especially today, which happened to be Bin Day. There's nothing quite like a line of wheelie bins to add that special something to a streetscape. But there's a charming quirk here: the streets running off the main drag are named after the days of the week — Monday Street, Tuesday Street and so on.

Take a turn off one of these "daily streets" and suddenly you're rewarded: a lovely lakeside reserve stretches along the water's edge, well maintained and peaceful. From here you can gaze out across the vast expanse of Tuggerah Lake, and on a clear day, you can just make out *The Entrance* across the water — where the lagoon meets the sea. Bird lovers would feel right at home here, with pelicans, swans and all sorts of waterbirds cruising by.

The houses backing onto the lakefront enjoy cracking views, but thankfully the reserve means the rest of us can share in the outlook too. It's a beautiful, calm spot perfect for a stroll or sitting quietly and just soaking up the serenity — one of those places where not much happens, but that's exactly the point.

Other than homes and the foreshore, there's not a huge amount going on. I spotted a small shopping centre with a handful of shops, the Koala Pre-School (complete with a giant inflatable Santa Express parked on the roof — love a bit of local festive cheer), and the Tuggerawong Progress Hall, which, judging by appearances, might not have progressed much lately.

All up, Tuggerawong won't knock your socks off with attractions, but it's a quietly lovely spot — ideal if you're looking for lakeside calm just a stone's throw from the bustle of The Entrance.

Fun Fact:

The name *Tuggerawong* is thought to come from an Aboriginal word meaning "cold place" or "cold winds" — not that it felt especially chilly today.

Must See:

- Tuggerah Lake foreshore reserve
- Birdwatching from the lakeside reserve
- The quirky daily street names

Key statistics:

- Population: approx. 1,600
- Location: western shore of Tuggerah Lake, NSW Central Coast
- Main vibe: residential, peaceful, lakeside living

CHAPTER 25
WOLLONDILLY (NSW)

Well, Wollondilly isn't a town in the usual sense — it's a shire made up of about 27 towns, villages, and locales. So, to do it justice (and avoid endless driving), I decided to head straight to the shire's 'capital' — *Picton*.

Picton is about 80 km south of Sydney and driving through its quiet streets felt like stepping back in time. Historic buildings line the road, with some charming old shops and homes giving the town a strong colonial-era vibe. One standout is *The George IV Inn*, built in 1839 and reputedly one of the oldest surviving hotel buildings in Australia. With the mercury pushing into the high 30s today, it was tempting to duck inside for a cold one, but curiosity won out — there were a couple of local landmarks I couldn't resist checking out first.

First stop: the *Picton Railway Viaduct* (officially the *Stonequarry Viaduct*), an impressive stone structure opened in 1863 that still carries trains across Stonequarry Creek today. A helpful signpost pointed me down a side street to a great vantage point. It's a beautiful old bridge, nestled in greenery, blending into the landscape as though it's always been part of it.

Picton, as it turns out, has a bit of a reputation when it comes to ghostly goings-on — one of the so-called hotspots for paranormal activity in Australia. Legend has it that people have drowned in Stonequarry Creek over the years and that splashing sounds can sometimes be heard when no one's around. Not today, though — the creek was mostly dry and eerily silent.

Next on my list was the old disused *Redbank Range Railway Tunnel*, known locally as the *Mushroom Tunnel*. This was the first railway tunnel used by NSW Railways when it opened in 1867, though it was retired from rail use by 1919 after a new line opened.

During WWII, the tunnel was pressed into service again — this time as a military storage site for ammunition and, apparently, mustard gas. After the war, it took on a far less dangerous role as a mushroom farm (hence the nickname), making it one of the more unusual reuses of wartime infrastructure I've come across.

Finding the tunnel wasn't entirely straightforward — my first attempt took me to the Picton underground reservoir instead — but before long, I was standing at the entrance. At 592 feet long, it's not hard to see daylight at the other end, and walking through in the middle of the day, it felt more interesting than creepy... though wearing sunglasses didn't exactly help my ability to see in the gloom (*doh!*).

I'm sure it'd feel much spookier on one of the *Ghost Hunts* that regularly visit the tunnel after dark — though, as I later learned, the tunnel is actually council property and legally only open Monday to Friday between 8 am and 2 pm. After hours, you're meant to view it only from the entry arch unless you're part of an authorised tour — fair enough, and probably worth knowing if you're planning a late-night wander.

Picton turned out to be a surprisingly fascinating place: a mix of history, charm, and ghost stories... all wrapped up in a peaceful country town atmosphere.

Fun Fact:

The *Mushroom Tunnel* was Australia's first railway tunnel and later stored everything from wartime munitions to commercial mushrooms — talk about a change in purpose.

Must See:

- The George IV Inn (one of Australia's oldest pubs)
- Stonequarry Viaduct
- The entrance to the Redbank Range Railway Tunnel (*aka* Mushroom Tunnel) — but check opening hours!
- Picton's heritage streetscapes and old buildings

Key statistics:

- Wollondilly Shire population: approx. 54,000
- Picton population: approx. 5,200
- Location: 80 km south-west of Sydney
- Known for: heritage buildings, ghost stories, railway history

CHAPTER 26
MITTAGONG (NSW)

After pulling into Picton for a quick break, I was bound for Canberra — but not before a couple of stops en route, the first being Mittagong.

Mittagong's a decent-sized town for this part of the world, with around 7,500 locals calling it home. It sits just off the old Hume Highway, so it's easy to detour in if you're following the classic inland route south.

This wasn't going to be a long visit — more of a "stick my nose in and see a couple of things" kind of stop — but Mittagong delivered.

First order of business: the Mittagong Lookout. A winding little road about 4 km out of town takes you up to this splendid vantage point where you can take in the whole spread — the town nestled in its wooded surrounds and rolling hills beyond. Follow the road a bit further and there are other lookouts too, offering cracking views in different directions. It's the sort of place where you can properly appreciate the scale of the Southern Highlands, with Mittagong looking like a sleepy toy town below.

But what really drew me in was something less polished and far more my style: the Old Maltings. Now I doubt these make the official Mittagong tourist trail, but there's always something strangely beautiful about a big derelict industrial building, and the Maltings didn't disappoint.

There are two large brick malthouses, sitting a few hundred metres apart — relics from the days when Tooth and Co., the old New South Wales brewing giant, ran the show here. Built from 1898, they were hard at work for decades before falling silent in the 1970s when brewing practices moved on and the site became surplus to requirements.

Today they stand as weathered, slightly eerie monuments to that industrial past: slate roofs still mostly intact, brickwork weathered but proud, and of course a healthy smattering of graffiti. It looked like someone had made a half-hearted go at renovating them not too long ago, but whatever plans there were clearly ran out of puff.

There's a real atmosphere about the place — decaying grandeur, you might call it — and for those who, like me, enjoy wandering around forgotten corners of history, it's magic.

Fun Fact:

Mittagong literally means "little mountain" in the local Dharawal language — a fitting name given the surrounding landscape.

Must See:

- Mittagong Lookout for those sweeping Highland vistas
- The hauntingly beautiful Old Maltings — bring your camera
- "Waratah" flowering in November.

Key Statistics:

- Location: Southern Highlands, New South Wales
- Population: Approx. 6,090
- Known for: Maltings, Southern Highlands charm, scenic lookouts

CHAPTER 27
BRINDABELLA (NSW)

The first destination of the day was Brindabella, sitting about 68 kilometres west of Canberra. With clear blue skies overhead, I was feeling optimistic as I set off. But that optimism got an early test. Just as I was reaching the peak of a hill, the smooth tarmac abruptly vanished — replaced without warning by a dusty dirt track.

You'd think, being so close to the nation's capital, they'd have sealed the road, but no. Had I bothered to consult a more detailed map, I would've known what I was in for — but where's the fun in that? Truth be told, the rough track didn't bother me much. Sure, the journey took longer, and the ride was a bit bumpier, but it added a sense of adventure.

Travelling a dirt road is refreshing at first, a novelty compared to the monotonous drone of the highway. The winding route climbed hills, hugged valleys, and offered glimpses of gum trees interspersed with firs. Wildlife was plentiful too — kangaroos bounced by, and at one point Amelie, my four-legged travel companion (a King Charles Spaniel with a strong sense of entitlement to smooth rides), and I spotted a strange black creature darting into the bush. It might have been a dog, maybe a dingo, possibly even a wolf... or, who knows, a four-legged Yeti. Let's just say I wasn't about to get out for a closer look.

Further along, we reached a spot called *Piccadilly Circus* — though unlike its bustling London namesake, this one consisted of nothing more than a junction of dusty tracks and a few tired signs. We passed a grand total of two vehicles the entire way.

But what of Brindabella itself? Well, this remote valley lies nestled within the northern reaches of the Australian Alps National Parks. It's rugged, scenic, and sparsely populated — a scattering of homesteads surrounded by vast bushland.

For a nature lover, there's plenty here to appreciate: mountains, forests, and the feeling of being somewhere far removed from the bustle of modern life. But for me, the real adventure was simply getting there. Like life itself, sometimes the journey's the whole point.

Fun Fact:

The Brindabella valley was once home to Australian author Miles Franklin, best known for her novel *My Brilliant Career*.

Must See:

- Brindabella National Park's lookout points and rugged alpine scenery
- The oddly named *Piccadilly Circus* — if only for a photo and a chuckle

- Wildlife spotting along the dirt tracks (kangaroos guaranteed; Yetis not so much)

Key Statistics:

- Location: Snowy Valleys Council and partly in Yass Valley Council
- Population: Approx. 22
- Known for: A large unpopulated area consisting of parts of the Brindabella National Park

CHAPTER 28
CANBERRA (ACT)

Canberra served as my base for exploring the surrounding region. I stayed in a comfortable little B&B tucked away in Aranda, and even Amelie (my travel companion of the furry, four-legged kind) was welcome — always a good start.

Canberra is full of attractions — so many that even a longer stay might not be enough to see it all properly. During my fleeting visit, I treated myself to the National Gallery of Australia, wandering amongst works by Van Gogh and Picasso, thanks to an exhibition on loan from the Musée d'Orsay. Honestly, standing there looking at those masterpieces — that alone made the visit worthwhile.

I've been to Canberra several times and I'll admit: I'm still trying to get my head around it. Having grown up in the UK and visited Europe's historic capitals, Canberra feels... different. For one, it's spacious. Where London squeezes itself into every available corner, Canberra seems to stretch itself out with ease. Traffic flows smoothly, lawns roll on endlessly, and you're more likely to find roundabouts and dual carriageways lined with gum trees than endless terraces.

And where most Aussies live a stone's throw from the sea, it's a good couple of hours to the nearest beach from here — something that almost feels un-Australian.

But Canberra's quirks come from the fact that it's a deliberately planned city. There are no ancient laneways or accidental corners; instead, it's neat, logical and impressively orderly — maybe even a little too perfect at times. It really is a capital designed by committee — which, of course, it was.

That's not to say it lacks soul — far from it. The museums here are world-class, and if you want to see Australia's democratic machinery up close (and marvel that it works at all), Parliament House is worth a look. Canberra just feels young, and perhaps with time it will acquire the character and quirks that come with age.

In the meantime, I'll happily enjoy it for what it is: green, peaceful, easy to get around — and with just enough kangaroos on the roads to keep you on your toes.

Fun Fact:

Canberra was chosen as Australia's capital as a compromise between rivals Sydney and Melbourne, with the exact location selected because it was roughly halfway between the two.

Must See:

- National Gallery of Australia
- Australian War Memorial

- Parliament House
- Lake Burley Griffin (perfect for a stroll or cycle)
- Mount Ainslie lookout (for cracking views over the city)

Key Statistics:

- Population: Approx. 473,000
- Location: Australian Capital Territory
- Nearest coast: ~150 km to Batemans Bay
- Known for: Politics, roundabouts, museums, and kangaroos in the suburbs

CHAPTER 29
CAPTAIN'S FLAT (NSW)

Captains Flat lies about 60 kilometres southwest of Canberra and was a place I was genuinely looking forward to — not for any grand natural wonder or cultural landmark, but because it lays claim to the longest bar in the southern hemisphere. If ever there was a reason to pop in for a beverage, that's it!

So naturally, I made a beeline for the Captains Flat Hotel, home of the famous bar. The barmaid was quick to fill me in on a bit of the venue's curious recent history: Apparently, the hotel had lost the title to Mildura some time ago... but Mildura's bar was later dismantled, meaning Captains Flat reclaimed the crown by default. Got to love a technical victory.

At first glance, I'll admit, the bar didn't strike me as particularly long — but then you notice how it loops around a corner and stretches through two rooms. Collectively, it's just long enough for the bragging rights. And certainly long enough for me and the two other punters quietly enjoying their drinks that afternoon.

Despite what the name might suggest, Captains Flat isn't flat at all — it's tucked into a hilly landscape that was once buzzing with gold miners back in the mid-1800s when generous seams of gold made this a thriving little town.

And as for the name itself? Well, there are a few theories, but I reckon the one shared on captainsflat.org is the best yarn:

Apparently, Foxlow Station nearby owned a gigantic white bullock called "Captain" who had a habit of dodging work and hiding on a favourite patch of river flat. Travelling drovers got so used to seeing this lazy beast there that they began calling the area Captain's Flat. Years later, Captain was found dead right on his favourite spot — now the town playing field. In true Aussie style, the locals honoured the beast rather than any man of rank. Sounds about right.

Fun Fact

Captains Flat was once home to one of Australia's largest lead and zinc mines, which operated until the 1960s — but it's the bullock that got the naming honours!

Must See

- Captains Flat Hotel – have a drink at the famous bar
- Captains Flat Heritage Walk – stroll the streets and take in remnants of its mining past
- Molonglo River – nearby river scenery for a picnic stop

Key Statistics

- Location: 60 km southwest of Canberra, NSW
- Population: Around 600
- Known for: Longest bar in the southern hemisphere, mining history

CHAPTER 30
JINDABYNE (NSW)

Jindabyne is a fascinating place to visit... when it's *not* snowing. And, I imagine, probably even more fun when it *is* snowing, given it's one of the main towns of the Snowy Mountains — so called, quite logically, because it actually snows there.

For my English readers: yes, it snows in Australia. Amazing, huh?

The official "season" kicks off in June, when the town goes into a frenzy preparing for the first falls. But visiting in March is still a pleasure — you get the alpine charm without the crowds (or the icy windburn). Jindabyne feels like an alpine resort gearing up for the main act. Shops are refitting or reopening after summer hibernation, while a few unlucky ones shut up for good, unable to survive the leaner months.

My hotel, despite being outside the peak season, had to double-check they had a room for me — thanks to a corporate conference full of Sydney office types looking to swap spreadsheets for fresh mountain air.

Jindabyne is surrounded by impressive mountains — part of the southern end of the Great Dividing Range, making it some of the coolest (literally) country in Australia. And then there's Lake Jindabyne, a large, gleaming body of water that completes the picture and keeps the town humming through summer too, thanks to boating, fishing and kayaking.

But here's a fascinating quirk: Jindabyne is one of three towns I've visited on this journey that had to relocate due to flooding. Only in this case, it wasn't a natural disaster — it was *planned*. When the Snowy Hydro Electricity Scheme was built, they needed to create Lake Jindabyne as a reservoir, so the old town was deliberately flooded. Some houses were physically moved to the town's new site on higher ground, overlooking the lake instead of sitting on its future bed.

And in a nice twist, during periods of drought, the remnants of old Jindabyne occasionally reappear from the depths — like ghosts of a drowned town, rising from the lake.

Wandering around Jindabyne felt like watching the dress rehearsal for a grand show. Everything's getting ready... just waiting for the curtain to rise when the snowflakes fall.

Fun Fact:

When water levels drop low enough during droughts, you can see the ruins of Old Jindabyne — including building foundations and roads — poking up from the lake bed.

Must See:

- Lake Jindabyne — perfect for fishing, sailing or a lakeside picnic

- Snowy Hydro Discovery Centre — learn the incredible history behind Australia's biggest hydroelectric scheme
- The main street — charming shops, alpine vibe, great cafes
- Use Jindabyne as a base for a day trip to Kosciuszko National Park

Key Statistics:

- Population: Approx. 2,600
- Location: Snowy Mountains, southern NSW
- Elevation: About 918 metres above sea level
- Known for: Ski season hub, Snowy Hydro Scheme, Lake Jindabyne

CHAPTER 31
ULLADULLA (NSW)

Just two hours after leaving Canberra I found myself on the New South Wales South Coast in the coastal town of Ulladulla — and straight away, it struck me as a town of two halves. The southern end had a definite industrial feel to it: car dealerships, machinery yards, and workshop-style businesses lining the roadside. But roll on into the northern end and things take a more relaxed, consumer-friendly turn: shopping strips, eateries, and easy access to the waterfront.

First stop: the tourist information centre, where I asked about *Pigeon House Mountain* — a local landmark I'd heard about. The mountain itself was apparently sighted by Captain Cook as he sailed up the coast and, thanks to its distinctive shape, he named it Pigeon House.

In recent years, though, it's been officially renamed *Didhol*, the original name used by the local Yuin people — *Didhol* being a reference to a part of the female anatomy the mountain is said to resemble. The lady behind the counter at the visitor centre, perhaps keen to preserve modesty, assured me it was better viewed as resembling a dromedary camel... so I think you get the general idea!

A quick five-minute detour took me to Kings Point, where I grabbed a photo of Didhol / Pigeon House Mountain from afar — impressive even at a distance.

Back in Ulladulla itself, I spent a pleasant hour or so strolling around: grabbing a bite to eat by the picturesque harbour, visiting the oldest house in town, and checking out the quirky lighthouse. This lighthouse deserves a mention because it's not perched dramatically on a cliff edge, but rather sitting in the middle of a roundabout at the end of a suburban street. Only in Australia.

And then there's the Marlin Hotel, which various guides claim as one of Ulladulla's "notable landmarks" thanks to the big fluorescent marlin on its roof. I hate to break it to anyone who's expecting something on par with the Big Banana or the Big Prawn... this marlin is small fry.

Overall, Ulladulla was a pleasant stop — part busy service town, part laid-back coastal getaway — and it felt like a nice place to pause before the next leg of the journey.

Fun Fact:

The name "Ulladulla" is thought to come from an Aboriginal word meaning "safe harbour" — fitting, given the sheltered port that remains the town's heart today.

Must See:

- Ulladulla Harbour

- Ulladulla lighthouse (yes, the one in the roundabout)
- Didhol / Pigeon House Mountain (best viewed from Kings Point)
- Oldest house in Ulladulla — a glimpse into early settlement days

Key statistics:

- Population: approx. 17,000
- Location: NSW South Coast
- Main industries: fishing, tourism, light industry

CHAPTER 32
UNANDERRA (NSW)

So far, this journey has delivered a string of fantastic places — all linked by nothing more than a mention in the lyrics of a song. From tiny country towns to the nation's capital, every stop has revealed something interesting or unexpected.

But I must admit... I approached Unanderra with a bit of trepidation after reading this rather uninspiring description beforehand:

"Unanderra has several local attractions, including a Kebab shop and an old school building in the Woolworths carpark."

Well, at least they were honest.

When I arrived, I was determined to give it a fair go and find something of interest but Unanderra felt like one of those suburbs where life just goes on quietly — not much fuss, but that's its charm. No quirky shops or grand old pubs, just an honest patch before continuing on my way to Wollongong.

But, as is often the case, it's what you discover later that can make a place more interesting. A bit of Googling after the fact revealed that Unanderra actually played an important role in post-war migration history. From the 1950s through the 1970s, Unanderra was home to a Government Hostel established to house newly arrived migrants — including many of the so-called "£10 Poms" who took up Australia's assisted passage scheme.

The hostel provided accommodation to help new arrivals settle into life in Australia and relieve refugee distress in the years following WWII. The Wollongong area was chosen because of the booming coal, iron and steel industries nearby, offering plentiful jobs and opportunities.

For many families, Unanderra was their first home on Australian soil — and judging by the stories on websites dedicated to the hostel's history, plenty of those families still look back on their time there with deep affection.

So, while I didn't find much to photograph or linger over on the day, Unanderra's story is actually quite significant — a reminder that sometimes the value of a place isn't in its scenery, but in its history.

Fun Fact:

Between 1951 and 1970, over a million migrants arrived in Australia under the assisted passage scheme — and many of them passed through hostels like the one at Unanderra.

Must See:

- Unanderra Railway Station (heritage listed and still in use)
- The Woolworths carpark (if you really want to spot that old school building!)
- If you're passing through, maybe hunt down that legendary kebab shop

Key statistics:

- Population: approx. 5,400
- Location: southern suburb of Wollongong, NSW South Coast
- Historically significant as a key migrant reception centre

CHAPTER 33
WOLLONGONG (NSW)

A short drive from Unanderra brought me to Wollongong — a coastal city whose name is believed to mean *"sound of the sea"* in the local Aboriginal language. And while it's a bustling regional hub these days — Australia's ninth-largest city, no less, with about 280,153 people — it's still got that salt-in-the-air coastal feel.

I'd read beforehand that Wollongong holds a unique coastal claim to fame: it's the only place on Australia's east coast where two lighthouses stand within spitting distance of each other. I was curious to see just how "close" they were.

After navigating a few suburban streets, I found myself at the beachside — and there was no mistaking the larger of the two: *Wollongong Head Lighthouse*, standing proudly at Flagstaff Hill. With fine weather and sweeping views, it was proving popular — families picnicking, walkers strolling — all while enjoying a vista that included, somewhat less romantically, a stretch of heavy industry to the south.

Just a short stroll down an incline brought me to the second: the smaller, older *Wollongong Breakwater Lighthouse* — affectionately known as the *Old Wollongong Lighthouse*. Built in 1871 and faithfully serving until 1974, this little lighthouse won the hearts of locals who now lovingly maintain and restore it, lighting it up only for special occasions. It's tucked neatly into the Belmore Basin at the end of the southern breakwater, a wonderful little pocket of history.

Wollongong also holds a more whimsical claim to fame: in the Harry Potter universe, it's home to the fictional professional Quidditch team, the *Woollongong Warriors* [sic]. Sadly, they only play in the pages of *Quidditch Through the Ages* by J.K. Rowling — no live matches to catch at the local oval.

And then, just for a laugh, there's the unforgettable nod from ABC's classic *Aunty Jack* version of *I've Been Everywhere*, which turns into a chant of "Wollongong" dozens of times over. If I'd been following *their* itinerary, I could have called it a day right here and simply stayed put — chanting "Wollongong" into the sunset!

Fun Fact:

Despite its industrial backdrop, Wollongong's beaches are some of the most popular surf spots in NSW — proof that you can combine heavy industry and beach culture in true Aussie style.

Must See:

- Wollongong Head Lighthouse at Flagstaff Hill
- Wollongong Breakwater Lighthouse in Belmore Basin

- The scenic coastline and harbour area

Key statistics:

- Population: approx. 280,000
- Location: NSW South Coast, about 85km south of Sydney
- Major industries: steelmaking, port operations, education, tourism

CHAPTER 34
GULGONG (NSW)

After a bit of a break since the last leg of my journey, it felt great to be back on the road visiting more "Everywhere" locations. This time, I drove 345 km from Terrigal along the Golden Highway to arrive at Gulgong — and what a town it is.

Let's wind the clock back to a rainy day on 14 April 1870. Somewhere along a sheep track, Tom Saunders, a humble sheep farmer, struck gold — literally. He spotted 14 ounces of gold that had washed to the surface. Word got out fast. By June, 500 hopeful diggers had arrived, and by 1872, Gulgong was booming, its population exploding to 20,000.

But like all gold rushes, this one didn't last long. By 1880, the rush had petered out. The town shrank to a fraction of its size and settled into a quieter life, with just over 2,200 residents today.

Yet the legacy of that gold rush remains vivid. Many Aussie country towns have that wild west movie vibe, but in Gulgong you hardly need to use your imagination — it's all still there. The unusually narrow streets, heritage buildings, timber verandas, old signage... it's a time capsule in the best sense. The town proudly boasts 170 historically significant buildings built between 1870 and 1910, and walking around feels like stepping back in time.

I had three "must-sees" on my list, starting with the brilliant Gulgong Pioneers Museum. What a surprise this was — it practically fills an entire block in the heart of town and offers an extraordinary collection thanks to the generosity of local donors. Inside are recreated rooms that bring rural life to life: a dentist's surgery, a hospital operating theatre, a bank, and even an old toy shop.

Outside, it just keeps going: farm machinery, a schoolhouse, a miner's cottage, and even a newspaper print shop. The place is vast. Honestly, you could spend a full day there and still not take it all in — it's well worth the visit.

Next on my list was the Prince of Wales Opera House. Built in 1870, it's Australia's oldest continually operating entertainment theatre. Now, I wasn't expecting a grand Sydney Opera House experience — and it isn't — but it oozes history and charm.

My real motivation? Dame Nellie Melba once performed here, back when she was known simply as Mrs Armstrong. And why do I care about that? Because it was in her honour that French chef Auguste Escoffier created *Peach Melba, Melba toast, Melba sauce and Melba garniture* — that's quite a legacy.

I couldn't resist asking at two local cafés whether they served Peach Melba, given this historic connection. Sadly, both owners looked at me as if I was "one peach short of a basket full."

Finally, I wanted to visit the Henry Lawson Centre, dedicated to Australia's famous novelist and bush poet who lived in Gulgong as a child while his father chased the dream of striking it rich. Unfortunately, it had closed earlier than its advertised hours — so I couldn't learn as much as I'd hoped. But I did know this: Henry Lawson sported one of the finest moustaches ever seen in Australian history.

His connection to Gulgong is celebrated proudly, especially as he appeared — along with Gulgong streetscapes — on the Australian $10 paper note from 1966 until 1993. The town embraces this bit of fame wholeheartedly, which I discovered when I booked into the Ten Dollar Town Motel. The name is cheeky, but sadly, the tariff was considerably more than $10!

In short, Gulgong is a cracker of a place. If you love local history, heritage architecture, museums, and charming country streets, this is absolutely worth a visit.

Fun Fact:

Gulgong proudly refers to itself as "Ten Dollar Town" due to its starring role on the Aussie $10 note from 1966 to 1993 — complete with images of Henry Lawson and Gulgong street scenes.

Must See:

- Gulgong Pioneers Museum — an incredible collection spread over an entire block
- Prince of Wales Opera House — Australia's oldest continuously operating theatre
- Stroll the narrow streets — full of original gold rush-era buildings and atmosphere

- Hunt down Gulgong's Henry Lawson connections — moustache optional

Key Statistics:

- Population: Approx. 2,200
- Location: Mid-Western NSW, part of the Mudgee region
- Elevation: About 300 metres above sea level
- Known for: Gold rush history, heritage streetscapes, Henry Lawson connections

CHAPTER 35
NARROMINE (NSW)

I must admit, I was a little slow off the mark this morning. The Gulgong motel receptionist cheerfully informed me I was the last guest to check out — but it was barely past 8:30 am, so I didn't feel too guilty for those few extra minutes under the covers.

Unfortunately, this was the day my luck with the weather ran out: drought-breaking rain pelted my windscreen along kilometre after kilometre of country roads. The ground, dry and parched from months of waiting, was soaking it up like a sponge. While some creeks were starting to brim, the roads remained passable — for now.

Despite the gloomy skies, there was a certain beauty to the landscape — red mud, dark thunderclouds, water pooling in the paddocks — and everywhere I went, locals were smiling. The rain, while a minor inconvenience for me, was cause for celebration for the farmers and countryfolk whose livelihoods depend on it. Walking the streets, I couldn't help but overhear cheerful comments about the long-awaited rain — it was headline news in every town.

So, what do you do on a wet morning in Narromine? The answer was obvious: visit the Narromine Aviation Museum.

Opened by legendary Australian aviatrix Nancy-Bird Walton in 2002, the museum is no dusty shed of relics — it's a modern, beautifully laid out tribute to Narromine's rich aviation heritage. The town's flying history goes back to the 1920s and it was home to Australia's first regional aero club. Today, Narromine remains a mecca for glider pilots from around the world thanks to its exceptional thermals.

When I visited, I had the place to myself — just me and the friendly volunteer guide on duty. And if you're lucky, like I was, your guide might offer to take you across the airfield for something a bit special.

I was invited to follow his car to an old 1940s hangar just a minute's drive away. The doors creaked open and at first, all I saw was darkness — but I could feel the excitement building. As I stepped inside, carefully over the big sliding hangar doors, I came face-to-face with a real treasure: Australia's only flying replica of a Wright Model A Flyer.

This beautiful machine first took to the skies of Narromine on 1 October 2005 — with none other than Buzz Aldrin himself there to witness it. For an entry fee of just $7 and a personal tour, this was an absolute bargain — and for me, the highlight of the day.

Sadly, thanks to the rain, I didn't get much chance to wander Narromine's town centre — though even in the downpour, I spotted a few hardy locals rushing about with umbrellas raised.

. . .

Fun Fact:

Narromine's Wright Model A Flyer replica is the only one in Australia that actually flies — and it was unveiled in style, with astronaut Buzz Aldrin present for its first flight.

Must See:

- Narromine Aviation Museum — superb exhibits on local aviation history
- Wright Model A Flyer replica — housed in an original 1940s hangar (ask the guide!)
- Narromine airfield — a key hub for gliding enthusiasts

Key Statistics:

- Population: Approx. 3,500
- Location: Central West NSW
- Elevation: About 195 metres
- Known for: Aviation history, Australia's first regional aero club, superb conditions for gliding

CHAPTER 36
TULLAMORE (NSW)

The rain kept bucketing down as I made my way from Narromine to Tullamore, with a fair stretch of the journey along unsealed track — always a bit more of an adventure when the weather turns. Nothing like a muddy back road to keep you alert behind the wheel.

Tullamore itself has worn a few names over the years. It started out as Bullock Creek back in 1870, then became Gobondery, before finally settling on Tullamore — thanks to a few Irish families from, you guessed it, Tullamore in Ireland. They named their property *Tullamore*, and the town decided that was as good a name as any.

The Irish influence runs deep here. As you roll into town, the first thing that jumps out is the sign for the Showgrounds — home of the annual Tullamore Irish Festival. With around 70–80% of the community claiming Irish ancestry, it's no surprise really. Names like Carey, Crowley, McAneney, Corcoran and property names like Omagh, Tralee, Ormonde and Kinvara dot the district. Even the town sign sports a big shamrock, just in case you missed the point.

I cruised through the quiet main street, lined with a modest clutch of shops. The Tullamore Hotel dominates the scene — far grander than you might expect for a town this size, as if it's waiting patiently for a crowd that never quite materialises (except, presumably, during the Irish Festival).

With the rain getting heavier and no obvious indoor attractions to duck into, there wasn't much else to do but drive around and soak up the atmosphere — figuratively, of course. The 680 locals were wisely tucked up indoors, so I didn't get a chance to experience the hospitality that helped Tullamore take out "Community of the Year" back in 2008.

A few photos later, it was back into the car and off again — the road ahead calling, and another song lyric destination ticked off the list.

Fun Fact:

The Tullamore Irish Festival is a key event in regional NSW, celebrating the area's strong Irish heritage with music, dance, food, and a good dose of craic.

Must See:

- Tullamore Showground (especially during the Irish Festival)
- The classic façade of the Tullamore Hotel
- Main street stroll — short but full of Irish heart

Key statistics:

- Population: approx. 680

- Location: Central West NSW
- Strong Irish heritage: around 70–80% of locals claim Irish ancestry

CHAPTER 37
MOLONG (NSW)

Molong was enjoying some much-needed rain when I called in — as was much of New South Wales. The town sign proudly announced its formation in 1822 and a population of 2,135... and I couldn't help but wonder who gets the job of updating that figure and how often they do it. Do they change it every time someone moves in or out?

Driving through town, it quickly became clear that most streets are quiet and residential, with everything centred around Bank Street — the main drag — which contains most of the shops and also many of the town's historic and most visually appealing buildings.

The name Molong comes from an Aboriginal word meaning "place of many rocks" — appropriate given the rocky ridges around the district.

Molong's growth really took off in the 1880s when it was announced that the western railway would be extended to the town, helping cement its place as a key service centre for the surrounding rural district.

Today, Molong sits at the heart of a productive farming region — producing wheat, sheep, wool, cattle, fruit and wine. A classic country town: small, tidy, and with just enough charm to make it a pleasant place for a quiet stop on the road.

Fun Fact:

Molong was once home to Yuranigh, an Aboriginal guide who accompanied explorer Sir Thomas Mitchell on his expeditions and was later honoured with a unique grave — one of the few Aboriginal men to be buried with both Aboriginal and European honours.

Must See:

- Bank Street — historic architecture and the heart of town life
- Local cafes and bakeries — for a pie or a coffee with a country feel
- The Molong Museum — if you have time to delve into local history

Key Statistics:

- Population: Approx. 2,135 (depending on when they last updated the sign!)
- Location: Central West NSW
- Elevation: Around 530 metres
- Known for: Historic Bank Street, farming district, "place of many rocks"

CHAPTER 38
LITHGOW (NSW)

I arrived late into Lithgow, following a scenic journey from Molong, but I was still keen to learn what makes this historic town tick — and why it uses a Big Miner's Lamp as its Tourist Information Centre.

Well, it turns out Lithgow is firmly at the heart of a coal mining district. There are two coal-powered power stations nearby (one of them the largest in New South Wales) and, true to form, plumes of steam and smoke can often be seen drifting over the surrounding Lithgow Valley. The valley itself was named by explorer John Oxley in honour of William Lithgow, NSW's first Auditor-General.

Lithgow's population today hovers around 20,000 and the town was once home to Australia's first commercially-viable steel mill. The site is now a tourist attraction called Blast Furnace Park — an evocative collection of industrial ruins that hint at Lithgow's gritty, working-class past.

But here's where things get unexpectedly interesting:

While researching what to see in Lithgow, I stumbled across a throwaway line on Wikipedia — "Lithgow was also the location of an alleged assassination attempt on the life of Queen Elizabeth II in 1970."

Now, *that* piqued my curiosity.

Apparently, this story only became public in January 2009 when retired Detective Superintendent Cliff McHardy, aged 81, finally spilled the beans. The tale goes like this:

On 29 April 1970, the Queen and the Duke of Edinburgh were travelling by train from Sydney to Orange, crossing the rugged Blue Mountains. Near Lithgow, as the royal train rounded a winding cutting, it struck a large log that had been deliberately wedged across the tracks. McHardy insisted this was a sabotage attempt, designed to derail the train and cause a catastrophic accident.

According to McHardy, disaster was narrowly averted because the driver happened to be going unusually slowly — which, knowing NSW trains, doesn't surprise me. Speed isn't a term I'd ever use to describe their generally glacial pace.

The log jammed under the front wheels and was dragged for about 200 metres before the train stopped safely at a level crossing. Despite the danger, the train was largely undamaged and the Queen and Duke, seemingly unaware of what had happened, continued their journey without incident.

Strange on two counts, really:

1. You'd think an alleged attempt to assassinate the Queen would have made bigger headlines at the time (it may have, but I certainly missed it), and

2. The idea that speed was a significant factor makes me chuckle — NSW trains rarely manage anything that could be described as "fast."

(On an unrelated but fun side note: Clontarf, a Sydney suburb, was the site of an unsuccessful assassination attempt on Queen Victoria's son, Prince Alfred, back in 1868 — Australia's first royal assassination attempt.)

Unfortunately, the relentless rain meant I didn't get to see as much of Lithgow as I would have liked — I had hoped to visit the famous Zig Zag Railway and the Glow Worm Tunnel. But they'll have to wait for another day, as it was time to press on to my next stop: Megalong.

Fun Fact:

Lithgow was the site of a little-known alleged assassination attempt on Queen Elizabeth II in 1970 — a log placed across the royal train's path was foiled by nothing more than the slow pace of a NSW train!

Must See:

- Blast Furnace Park — atmospheric ruins of Australia's first steelworks
- Zig Zag Railway — historic switchback railway (next time for me!)
- Glow Worm Tunnel — popular bush walk and unique attraction in an old railway tunnel
- Big Miner's Lamp — iconic entry to Lithgow's visitor centre

Key Statistics:

- Population: Approx. 20,000
- Location: Western edge of the Blue Mountains, NSW
- Elevation: About 950 metres above sea level
- Known for: Coal mining history, steelworks heritage, rugged scenery

CHAPTER 39
MEGALONG (NSW)

Megalong is one of those places where the journey there is arguably more rewarding than the destination itself — and that's perfectly fine.

Driving from Lithgow to Megalong means winding your way through the Blue Mountains, part of the majestic Great Dividing Range. With the extra altitude came the coldest part of the trip so far — the temperature had dipped to a positively brisk 16°C (for Aussies, that's practically Antarctic!) and a good dose of fog added to the atmosphere.

But going down into the Megalong Valley — now *that* was something special. The road twists and turns through hairpin bends, hugs steep cliff faces, dodges roadside waterfalls, plunges into pockets of thick vegetation and demands your attention at every incline and descent. It's the kind of drive where you keep one eye on the scenery and the other firmly on the brakes.

Eventually, after a thrilling descent, my GPS proudly

announced that I'd arrived at my destination... and well, there wasn't much there to greet me.

Megalong itself is less a "town" and more a peaceful rural outpost, home to just 164 residents who are scattered across rural properties. The centrepiece of this "hub" is — quite literally — a single tea shop.

But that's kind of the charm. The Megalong Valley is less about attractions and more about the serenity, the landscape, and the journey itself. The isolation, the cool air, the towering escarpments — it all feels like a world away from city life.

And honestly, a quiet cup of tea at the valley's one café while looking out over the dramatic scenery isn't the worst way to spend an afternoon.

Fun Fact:

The name "Megalong" comes from an Aboriginal word believed to mean "Valley Under the Rock" — an apt description for this peaceful place nestled beneath towering sandstone cliffs.

Must See:

- The drive itself — one of the most scenic descents into a valley you'll find in NSW
- The lone tea shop — reward yourself at the end of the winding road
- Surrounding bush walks — this is Blue Mountains country after all

Key Statistics:

- Population: Approx. 164
- Location: Blue Mountains region, NSW
- Elevation: Approx. 500 metres in the valley floor, surrounded by much higher escarpments
- Known for: Dramatic drive, stunning scenery, tranquil vibe — and its tea shop!

CHAPTER 40
KURRAJONG (NSW)

After a pleasant wander through the Blue Mountains, weaving up and down foggy roads, I soon arrived at my next stop: Kurrajong — and, more specifically, the Kurrajong Radio Museum.

Yes, we do have fog in Australia too!

The museum promised a fascinating dive into radio history and is run by Ian O'Toole (call sign VK2ZIO). Sadly, despite arriving at 10:20 am with an "OPEN" sign clearly on display, I rang the bell... and waited... and waited... but no one came to let me in. Perhaps Ian was out fine-tuning his antennas.

Not to be deterred, I headed a little further down the hill to grab my customary photo beside the "Kurrajong" town sign and took a moment to enjoy the sounds of the bellbirds — and oddly enough, a few goats thrown in for good measure.

Turning off the Bells Line of Road, I found myself in the village of Kurrajong proper — a pretty little place with well-spaced homes nestled among greenery, and a small but well-stocked shopping centre. It had a relaxed, country feel, tucked away from the hustle and bustle.

The Bells Line of Road itself is worth a mention. In the early days, European settlers struggled to cross the daunting Blue Mountains until William Lawson, Gregory Blaxland, and William Charles Wentworth made their historic crossing in 1813, paving the way for the Great Western Highway — now the major road heading west.

But Archibald Bell carved out an alternative route a decade later in 1823, after tracking Aboriginal women escaping a kidnap by the Springwood tribe. His path eventually became a rough stock route and by 1841, convict labour had constructed a more usable track through Kurrajong.

The road we drive today — with gentler gradients and sealed surfaces — was opened in 1901 and improved again during WWII. This route still bears its rather formal name: "Bells Line of Road".

And with Kurrajong, I wrapped up another leg of my journey — with 9,910 km clocked since setting off, it was time to head back home to Terrigal.

Fun Fact:

The Bells Line of Road follows a path that owes its discovery to a very human story: Archibald Bell followed Aboriginal women escaping their captors — and unwittingly laid the groundwork for one of NSW's key mountain routes.

Must See:

- Kurrajong Radio Museum — if you're luckier than me and actually find it open!
- Bells Line of Road — a scenic and historic drive through the Blue Mountains
- Stroll the village — relaxed, green, and full of small-town charm

Key Statistics:

- Population: Approx. 3,000
- Location: Hawkesbury region, NSW, at the foothills of the Blue Mountains
- Elevation: About 500 metres above sea level
- Known for: Scenic drives, proximity to nature, bellbirds — and goats!

CHAPTER 41
TURRAMURRA (NSW)

Every time I head into Sydney, I drive straight through Turramurra — but thanks to this project, today I finally had reason to stop and have a proper look around.

First impressions? Well... if you're arriving via the Pacific Highway, you're greeted by the roar and colour of endless traffic. The highway slices right through the middle of the suburb and even outside peak hour, the traffic noise is pretty relentless. Not exactly postcard stuff.

But — and there's always a but — turn off that main drag and you quickly discover a very different side to Turramurra. Leafy lanes, hilly streets, and peaceful little pockets that almost make you forget that chaotic highway just a block away.

The heart of Turramurra is essentially a few shopping streets running off the Pacific Highway, along with the shops lining the highway itself. Beyond that, it's classic Sydney suburbia — mainly residential streets, home to workers who commute to the city. Turramurra is definitely a dormitory suburb rather than a tourist hotspot, but that's not to say there's no charm here.

In fact, I stumbled upon a few nice surprises: a quality antique shop, some restaurants that look worth a visit, and a quirky little garden centre smack bang in the middle of the shopping strip. There's not much in the way of typical tourist attractions, but a bit of pre-visit research revealed that Turramurra has had more than its fair share of notable residents over the years, including:

- Chris Lilley (of *Summer Heights High* fame)

- Kamahl (the legendary crooner)

- Hugh Jackman (Hollywood royalty)

- Grace Cossington Smith (renowned Australian painter)

- Gretel Killeen (former *Big Brother* presenter)

So if you're feeling playful, you could always spend an afternoon hunting down the homes of the famous, or simply wander the suburb's collection of lovely period properties. One standout is *Ingleholme*, a beautiful two-storey Federation house in Boomerang Street, built in 1896 by architect John Sulman — the man who left his mark on the design of Canberra.

After a leisurely wander through the leafy streets and a bit of daydreaming about living in a grand Federation home, it was time to wrap up my visit. Turramurra may not be a destination you'd travel far to see, but there's always something satisfying about slowing down and exploring a suburb you've so often just driven straight through.

. . .

Fun Fact:

The name *Turramurra* is thought to come from an Aboriginal word meaning "high hill" or "small watercourse" — both quite fitting given the suburb's elevated position and leafy character.

Must See:

- Federation homes and leafy streets
- *Ingleholme* on Boomerang Street
- The quirky garden centre in the middle of town
- Antique browsing on the main strip

Key statistics:

- Population: approx. 12,000
- Location: Upper North Shore, Sydney
- Main vibe: residential, leafy, quiet pockets off a busy highway

CHAPTER 42
NARRABEEN (NSW)

Today's outing took me from Terrigal down to Sydney to tick off a couple more "Everywhere" locations. First stop: Narrabeen, a beachside suburb that, to me, typifies the classic Sydney city beach.

Narrabeen boasts not just one beach but three — North Narrabeen, Narrabeen and South Narrabeen — each offering ample sea and sand, and in the case of North Narrabeen, one of the world's great surf breaks. Naturally, each beach comes complete with its own Surf Life Saving Club, cafés and plenty of homes and units to house the many who've chosen the beachside life.

Of course, being a city beach, it's not exactly tranquil. The roar of the waves competes with the buzz of Pittwater Road and its endless traffic.

But Narrabeen holds a darker, more fascinating tale too. Enter the Octavia Street bus stop...

Now, before I arrived, I'd read about an incident that took place right here — and although I didn't bring a deerstalker hat or a pipe, I did have my faithful Cavalier King Charles Spaniel **Amelie** with me, ready to sniff out clues in true Sherlock Holmes fashion.

On first glance, the bus stop on the corner of Octavia and Ocean Streets looked perfectly ordinary — just a spot where locals might wait for a ride into town. But beneath this seemingly innocent scene lies a story that stretches back thousands of years.

In January 2005, contractors digging a trench for electricity cabling made a shocking discovery: the skeletal remains of an Aboriginal man, approximately 183 cm (6 feet) tall, aged between 30–40 years at death.

Further investigation revealed this was no ordinary burial. The man had suffered a violent death, with a spear tip embedded in his spine, another spear lodged from behind, and a third wound to his skull. Nearby evidence suggested more spears had struck their mark but didn't damage the bones. Even his last meal was revealed — tiny fish bones still present in his stomach.

Who killed this man? No one knows. But what amazed archaeologists most was when this all happened: radiocarbon dating showed that this grim encounter occurred over 4,000 years ago.

The victim, now known as "Narrabeen Man", is the oldest dated skeleton ever discovered in Sydney. And despite the forensic attention he received after discovery in 2005, he's since been respectfully reburied in Ku-ring-gai Chase National Park.

As Amelie and I wandered back to the car, I pondered this extraordinary find hidden beneath an unremarkable suburban bus stop. Judging from the glint in her eye, Amelie was simply wondering if there were any bones left...

Fun Fact:

"Narrabeen Man" is estimated to be over 4,000 years old — the oldest skeleton found in Sydney — and his violent death has intrigued archaeologists and historians since his discovery.

Must See:

- North Narrabeen surf break — one of the world's great surf spots
- Narrabeen's beaches and headlands — perfect for a stroll or picnic
- Site of the Octavia Street bus stop — where "Narrabeen Man" lay undisturbed for millennia

Key Statistics:

- Population: Approx. 8,000
- Location: Northern Beaches, Sydney, NSW
- Elevation: Sea level, right on the Pacific coast
- Known for: Surf culture, Narrabeen Lagoon, rich Aboriginal history

CHAPTER 43
COLLAROY (NSW)

After a wander through Narrabeen, it was just a short drive to Collaroy — though honestly, it's hard to tell where one ends and the other begins. The two suburbs share the same stretch of beach, the same line of shops along Pittwater Road, and the same slightly chaotic traffic that barrels its way up and down this main northern artery.

But here's where things get interesting. Until the early 1900s, Collaroy didn't even officially exist — it was simply part of Narrabeen. All that changed thanks to a shipwreck that must have caused quite a stir back in the day.

In the early hours of 20 January 1881, the steamship *S.S. Collaroy*, built in Liverpool way back in 1859, managed to run itself ashore here in thick fog. Not just for a day or two either — it stayed stuck in the sand for three long years before they finally hauled it off again in 1884. That event was apparently so memorable the locals decided the area needed a new name: *Collaroy* it became.

The poor old *S.S. Collaroy* didn't have a lucky life though — it eventually came to grief again, this time far from Sydney, breaking up in fog off the Californian coast in 1889 while hauling a cargo of redwood destined for Sydney.

These days, Collaroy is a breezy beachside suburb that blends seamlessly with Narrabeen. A row of shops and cafés hug Pittwater Road and beyond that is the beach — always ready for locals and visitors alike. Not much separates the two places except history and a name inspired by that unfortunate steamer.

Fun fact:

The *S.S. Collaroy* wasn't the last ship to come to grief in these waters — Collaroy Beach remains a hotspot for surfing... and the occasional dramatic coastal swell!

Must See:

- Collaroy Beach — a perfect spot for swimming or just lazing about watching the waves
- Collaroy Cinema — a charming little cinema that's been part of the community for generations
- Long Reef Headland — just to the south, this scenic headland offers sweeping coastal views and walking trails

Key statistics:

- Population: Around 7,800
- Location: Northern Beaches, about 22 km north of Sydney CBD

- Known for: Beautiful beach, relaxed coastal vibe, and of course, the shipwreck that gave it its name

CHAPTER 44
KIRRIBILLI (NSW)

Kirribilli is very much a *Sunday* kind of suburb. If you find yourself in Sydney on a lazy Sunday morning, popping across to Kirribilli is a fine way to start the day — a wander through the regular markets held under the Harbour Bridge, maybe a spot of brunch at one of the many street-side cafés, all enjoyed at a wonderfully unhurried pace.

I found Kirribilli refreshing. There's a calmness in the air here that's a world away from the hubbub of Sydney's Central Business District just across the water. The streets are leafy, the atmosphere laid-back — but if you want action, you only need to look up.

Venture up a nearby flight of concrete steps and you're transported instantly to another world: above you looms the mighty Sydney Harbour Bridge, and before you, the city skyline and iconic Opera House. The noise of traffic fills the air and you suddenly appreciate just how impressive this structure is.

In fact, depending on how you look at it, the Harbour Bridge either starts or ends in Kirribilli. Whichever way you think of it, it's impossible not to be awed standing beneath its steel arch as eight lanes of traffic, trains, and cyclists hurtle across what is officially the world's widest long-span bridge.

Locals affectionately call it "The Coathanger" for obvious reasons. The road that crosses it is named the John Bradfield Highway, after the chief engineer who made the bridge happen. Bradfield's design was inspired by New York's Hell Gate Bridge, but the Sydney version — grander and far more famous — opened in 1932.

When it opened, tolls were just sixpence for a car or threepence for a horse and rider. Those days are long gone. The tolls have risen steadily over the years (and are now charged in only one direction — into the city, not out). The bridge was officially "paid off" by 1988, but tolls continue today to fund ongoing maintenance. A small price to pay for a national icon.

Kirribilli also has a rather exclusive feel — and with good reason. It's home to Kirribilli House, the official Sydney residence of the Prime Minister, and Admiralty House, official residence of the Governor-General when in town.

Former PM John Howard was famous not just for living here but also for his early morning walks around the suburb — complete with the daggy attire he made his own (tracksuit and white sneakers, naturally).

It's hard not to feel like you're walking through a privileged pocket of Sydney when you stroll around Kirribilli, but it retains a welcoming charm. The mix of grand residences, harbour-side parks, leafy streets and buzzing little cafés means it's a suburb where anyone can feel at home — at least for a lazy Sunday morning.

Fun Fact:

The toll for crossing the Harbour Bridge when it opened in 1932 was 6 pence for a car — and 3 pence for a horse and rider. Today, it costs a fair bit more (especially if you're still riding a horse).

Must See:

- Kirribilli Markets — vibrant and held regularly under the bridge
- Sydney Harbour Bridge views — climb those steps and enjoy the spectacle
- Stroll along Broughton Street for quaint cafés and harbour glimpses
- Snap a photo of Kirribilli House (from outside the gate, of course!)

Key Statistics:

- Population: Approx. 4,000
- Location: Lower North Shore of Sydney, just across from Circular Quay
- Elevation: Low-lying, right on Sydney Harbour
- Known for: Sydney Harbour Bridge, Kirribilli House, leafy streets and markets

CHAPTER 45
WOOLLOOMOOLOO (NSW)

You've got to admit, *Woolloomooloo* is one of the best place names going around. It practically demands a grin and sparks curiosity about what the suburb itself might actually be like.

As for what *Woolloomooloo* means, well... the jury's still out. Depending on who you ask, it either translates as "place of plenty" or "young black kangaroo" — both perfectly fine interpretations for such a quirky name.

This inner-Sydney suburb is just a stone's throw from the city centre and has an interesting history. Traditionally, Woolloomooloo was a working-class district — a bit rough around the edges — but these days it's a different story. Sure, there are still housing commission flats, but it's also home to the well-heeled and even a few celebrities. Russell Crowe, for instance, owns a $14 million penthouse apartment on the iconic Finger Wharf.

Speaking of the wharf — *Finger Wharf* itself is an impressive sight. It's the largest wooden structure in the world, stretching a whopping 400 metres long and 63 metres wide, standing on an incredible 3,600 timber piles. You can't help but admire it — a reminder of Sydney's maritime heritage now reborn as a swanky residential and dining precinct.

But arguably Woolloomooloo's most famous institution isn't the wharf, a gallery, or even a theatre... it's a humble pie shop. And not just any pie shop — this is *Harry's Café de Wheels*, a true Sydney icon.

Since 1938 (with a wartime break in the middle), Harry's has been serving up legendary pies, attracting everyone from Frank Sinatra, Marlene Dietrich and Robert Mitchum to Kerry Packer, Richard Branson and Pamela Anderson. Even Russell Crowe, when he's not kicking back in his penthouse, has been known to pop down for a pie.

The café's quirky name comes courtesy of the city council of the day, who ruled that mobile food caravans had to move at least 12 inches every day to avoid being classed as a permanent fixture. Harry duly obliged — rolling his caravan just enough to comply — and so it became *Harry's Café de Wheels*. Before that? It was simply "Harry's".

So while Woolloomooloo might be a mix of gritty history and gentrified glamour these days, it still knows how to keep things wonderfully down to earth — especially if you're hungry.

Fun Fact:

Woolloomooloo's Finger Wharf is so large it once handled multiple ocean liners at once — today, it's lined with upmarket apartments and restaurants (plus the odd celebrity resident!).

Must See:

- *Finger Wharf* — the largest timber-piled structure in the world
- *Harry's Café de Wheels* — grab a famous pie and peas
- Stroll the historic streets with their mix of old terraces and shiny new developments

Key statistics:

- Population: approx. 4,000
- Location: Inner Sydney, east of the CBD
- Known for: Finger Wharf, Harry's Café de Wheels, colourful history

CHAPTER 46
CARINGBAH (NSW)

I reckon it's fair to say that Caringbah isn't exactly on the tourist map. Tucked away in Sydney's Sutherland Shire, it feels more like a practical sort of place — a collection of residential streets, light industry and commercial strips, all seemingly there to house and service those working in the big smoke.

As a wandering tourist, there wasn't much to hold my attention here. The main drag is a busy road lined with shops you'll see in just about every other Aussie high street — national chains and a fair few small factories thrown in for good measure. Blink and you'd think you were in any one of Sydney's suburban corridors. The residential pockets sit further back from the bustle, quietly doing their thing.

Interestingly, the place was originally called *Highfield*, but that name didn't stick. When the post office opened in 1912, it was renamed to *Caringbah*, drawn from an Aboriginal word for a *pademelon wallaby*.

From the 1880s until just after WWII, this whole district was mostly market gardens feeding hungry Sydneysiders, so it doesn't have the deep colonial history or sandstone charm of inner Sydney. In many ways, Caringbah is a relative newcomer still finding its character.

But it does have a claim to fame, of sorts — this is where Lara Bingle was born. Yep, *that* Lara Bingle, who shot to fame as the face of the Australian tourism campaign that asked: *"Where the bloody hell are you?"* While her life later attracted a bit of tabloid fodder (thanks to a certain footballer and some rather private shower photos), it's that tourism ad that most folks would remember — filmed not in Caringbah, but up the coast at Fingal Spit... which, truth be told, would probably be a bigger drawcard for any tourist than a day wandering around Caringbah!

Fun Fact:

The name *Caringbah* comes from the Dharawal language word for the small wallaby known as a pademelon — though your odds of spotting one here today are pretty slim!

Must See:

- Westfield Miranda shopping centre nearby if you fancy a retail fix.
- Cronulla Beach is a short drive east if you want to swap factories for surf.

Key Statistics:

- Population: Approx. 11,000
- Location: 24 km south of Sydney CBD
- Local government area: Sutherland Shire

CHAPTER 47
ENGADINE (NSW)

You've got your country towns, you've got your city suburbs... and then you've got Engadine, which is a bit of a hybrid of the two. When I rolled into town on a Sunday morning, I half-expected the usual country town quiet — shutters down, streets empty, maybe a few blokes loitering near the pub. But Engadine surprised me.

Sure, it *looks* like a country town — everything's neat and tidy, the streets are spacious and there's that relaxed, laid-back vibe — but here were people out and about, shops actually open, and a general air of quiet bustle. A suburb pretending to be a country town, or maybe the other way around.

I had my trusty companion Amelie, my Cavalier King Charles Spaniel, with me as we wandered down the high street. Amelie took a keen interest in a display of stuffed cats and dogs outside a shop, thoroughly inspecting them as only a spaniel can.

A Scottish lady stopped for a chat — well, really to introduce herself to Amelie — and told me all about her breeding of

Scottie dogs. Apparently, some Scottish celebrity owns one of her dogs' offspring. Unfortunately, the celebrity's name meant nothing to me, so that bit of gossip was lost in translation.

The town centre itself is modest — a butcher, a newsagent, a chemist — just the essentials really, and mostly modern. This wasn't always a suburban hub, though. Originally, the area was all grazing land, and being close to Sydney, it became popular with campers and day-trippers looking to escape the city for a while.

That all changed in the 1920s when the railway arrived, giving Engadine better connections and slowly shifting its character. The post office opened in 1927, the first school in 1932, and by the 1960s it was firmly on its way to becoming a residential suburb.

The name Engadine itself isn't Aboriginal — which makes it a bit unusual for this part of the world — but is instead borrowed from the Engadin Valley in Switzerland. This nod to Switzerland came courtesy of Charles McAlister, who bought much of the land in 1890 after returning from a trip there. Slightly awkwardly, the land he purchased had actually been reserved for a national park in 1879, so there was probably a bit of controversy around that at the time.

Today, Engadine still feels a bit picturesque, hemmed in on one side by the beautiful Royal National Park — Australia's first national park — and on the other side by Lucas Heights, where, to my surprise, the Australian Nuclear Science and Technology Organisation operates a fully-fledged nuclear reactor. Just your typical suburb: butcher, baker, nuclear reactor...

. . .

Fun Fact:

The Royal National Park, right next door to Engadine, is the second-oldest national park in the world, after Yellowstone in the USA.

Must See:

- High Street — small but charming, with friendly locals and a country-town feel
- The edge of the Royal National Park — a perfect spot for a bush-walk
- Lucas Heights (at least to ponder the strangeness of a nuclear reactor just down the road)

Key Statistics:

- Population: Approx. 17,000
- Location: Southern Sydney, NSW
- Elevation: Around 200 metres
- Known for: Its unique country-meets-suburbia vibe, proximity to the Royal National Park, and its neighbour Lucas Heights nuclear facility

CHAPTER 48
MILPERRA (NSW)

Milperra is one of those suburbs that's probably best described as *not* being on the tourist route. It's a backroom kind of place — where people live, work, go about their daily business, but don't necessarily spruce up the neighbourhood to charm visitors.

It feels a bit too young to have much in the way of heritage buildings or quaint history, and most visitors here are probably heading to the local college, getting their muffler or tyres sorted, or just passing through on the way somewhere else. That's not a criticism — suburbs like Milperra play an essential role, providing the practical services and housing that help keep a big city running smoothly.

The name Milperra comes from an Aboriginal word meaning "gathering of people". Sadly, it's this idea of gathering that has made Milperra infamous in Australian history.

On Father's Day, 2 September 1984, Milperra was the scene of what became known as the Milperra Massacre. What started as a peaceful British motorcycle swap meet at the Viking

Tavern turned violent when two rival motorcycle gangs, the Comancheros and Bandidos, arrived. The two gangs lined up at opposite ends of the car park and, after a signal from the Comancheros' founder, all hell broke loose. Within minutes, four Comancheros, two Bandidos, and tragically, a 14-year-old innocent bystander were dead. Another 28 people were wounded, with 20 requiring hospitalisation.

Even with over 200 police officers attending, it took them ten minutes to bring the scene under control. It was one of the bloodiest days in modern Australian criminal history, and led to one of the country's largest ever court cases:

- 43 people charged with seven counts of murder
- 7 Comancheros received life sentences
- 16 Bandidos served 14 years for manslaughter

The Viking Tavern itself was later renovated, rebuilt, rebranded, and landscaped — today it's simply called The Mill.

It's a heavy chapter in Australian history and one this peaceful suburb carries quietly today. Thankfully, Milperra has happier claims to fame too — Olympic champion Ian Thorpe, Australia's legendary swimmer, was born here. Not a bad claim to fame for a suburban backroom.

Fun Fact:

Ian Thorpe, Australia's most decorated Olympian, was born in Milperra — proof that even the most unassuming suburbs can produce national legends.

Must See:

- The Mill (former Viking Tavern) — quietly rebuilt, with no obvious signs of its dark past
- Milperra's residential streets — typical working suburb, no-frills but essential
- Local cafés — simple spots for a cuppa away from the hustle of Sydney

Key Statistics:

- Population: Approx. 3,800
- Location: South-western Sydney, NSW
- Elevation: About 20 metres above sea level
- Known for: Site of the Milperra Massacre, birthplace of Ian Thorpe, practical suburban life

CHAPTER 49
CABRAMATTA (NSW)

I rolled into Cabramatta on an overcast Sunday afternoon, but the grey skies didn't seem to matter — the place was absolutely buzzing. Chinese lanterns lined the high street, Asian grocery stores spilled their colourful produce onto the pavement, and the smells of international cuisine wafted through the air. It's no wonder Cabramatta is nicknamed *Little Asia*.

Most big cities have their token Chinatown, but Cabramatta goes well beyond that — it actually feels like being *in* Asia. If I ever fancy a quick Asian getaway without leaving Australia, I reckon a day in Cabramatta would do the trick. With people from over 120 countries living and working here, it's arguably even more diverse than visiting any single country in Asia. In fact, they even offer "Day Trip to Asia" tours — not a bad idea if you're just popping in for the afternoon.

As I wandered from my car towards the heart of town, I passed groups sitting comfortably on milk crates on patches of grass in front of their flats, chatting and watching the world go by. But the laid-back vibe gave way quickly to a hive of activity as I reached the supermarkets and shops. Here, it felt like all of Cabramatta was out shopping for dinner and catching up on the latest gossip — the energy was infectious.

Curious as ever, I looked into the suburb's backstory. The name 'Cabramatta' itself has Aboriginal origins — 'Cabra' referring to a tasty water grub, and 'Matta' meaning a point or jutting piece of land. But how did this corner of Sydney come to feel more like Saigon or Hanoi than suburban Australia?

It turns out that a migrant hostel played a pivotal role. In the 1950s and 60s, post-war European immigrants came through the area in large numbers, setting up homes and businesses. But it was the second wave, during the 60s and 70s, that really defined Cabramatta's character — with large numbers of migrants arriving from South-East Asia after the Vietnam War. This transformed the suburb into the thriving multicultural hub we see today, while gently nudging aside the legacy of earlier European settlers.

Of course, Cabramatta's history isn't without its darker chapters. The suburb was once infamous for crime, drugs, and even made national headlines in 1994 when NSW State MP John Newman was assassinated outside his home here — Australia's first political assassination — at the hands of nightclub owner and political rival Phuong Ngo. Back then, Cabramatta Railway Station was grimly nicknamed the "smack express".

Thankfully, those days seem largely behind it, and today Cabramatta is a vibrant, welcoming and utterly unique community. Its multicultural heart beats strongly — and it's well worth a visit just to experience firsthand how different cultures have come together to create something uniquely Australian.

Fun Fact:

Cabramatta's Pho restaurants are considered by many to serve up the best bowls of pho in Australia — a claim you'd have to settle yourself, spoon in hand!

Must See:

- Stroll along John Street for authentic Asian eateries and shops
- Visit Freedom Plaza and its iconic friendship arch
- Explore the bustling Cabramatta markets
- Stop for a photo at the colourful murals dotted around town

Key Statistics:

- Population: approx. 22,000
- Location: 30 km south-west of Sydney CBD
- Languages spoken: Vietnamese is the most common language other than English

CHAPTER 50
PARRAMATTA (NSW)

Driving into Parramatta, it quickly became clear I wasn't arriving in a sleepy country town. The high-rise office blocks lining the skyline signalled loud and clear that Parramatta is no ordinary suburb — it's a major city within the Sydney metropolitan sprawl.

And with that status come all the usual trappings: rows of used car lots, massive shopping centres, parking meters everywhere, and traffic — lots of traffic. Compared to some of the small towns and villages I'd visited earlier on this journey, Parramatta felt like a concrete maze — a place that runs on a strict timetable and seems to work best between 9 to 5, Monday to Friday.

But beneath all the hustle, there's an important history waiting to be uncovered.

I won't dwell on the shopping malls or the packed high street. Instead, let's step back in time to why Parramatta exists at all — and why it came into being so soon after the arrival of the First Fleet.

Just seven months after Sydney Cove was established, the British realised they had a problem: Sydney's soil wasn't up to much when it came to growing food. So the search was on for more fertile ground — and they found it where Parramatta now stands. Good farming land, a river providing easy transport back to Sydney, and the bonus that the Parramatta River turned fresh at this point made it the perfect spot for the new farming settlement.

Within two years, the town was taking shape, and by 1791 around 552 inhabitants (500 of them convicts!) were calling this place home. Originally named "Rose Hill", the town soon became known as Parramatta — a name that stuck.

By the early 1800s, Parramatta had hospitals, schools, churches and a raft of public buildings, quickly becoming both an army town and an important centre of colonial government.

Before I left, I couldn't help but reflect on one colourful tale from the early days — the story of Joseph Samuel.

In 1801, Joseph was transported to Australia for robbery, but not long after arriving, he found himself in deeper trouble — accused of being part of a gang that robbed a wealthy woman's home, during which a police officer was killed.

Joseph admitted to the robbery but denied the murder. Nevertheless, he was sentenced to hang. What happened next is the stuff of legend:

- On the first attempt, the rope broke.

- On the second attempt, the noose slipped off his neck.

- On the third attempt, the new rope broke again.

The gathered crowd was in an uproar, and the spectacle was so extraordinary that Governor Phillip was called in and pardoned Joseph on the spot, interpreting the events as divine intervention.

You can't make this stuff up.

It was getting late by the time I finished my brief visit, but Parramatta is one of those places I'll need to return to — to explore the river, learn more of its fascinating past, and see how this city-within-a-city continues to evolve.

Fun Fact:

Joseph Samuel's failed hanging in 1803 is believed to be Australia's first case of a "miraculous escape from execution", earning him the nickname *the man they couldn't hang*.

Must See:

- Parramatta River foreshore — perfect for a stroll and a glimpse of the city's historic heart
- Old Government House — Australia's oldest surviving public building
- Parramatta Park — a tranquil green space in the heart of this busy city

Key Statistics:

- Population: Approx. 260,000 (making it one of Australia's largest urban centres)
- Location: Western Sydney, NSW, about 23 km from the Sydney CBD

- Elevation: Around 14 metres
- Known for: Major business district, colonial history, multicultural community

CHAPTER 51
GIRRAWEEN (NSW)

Driving into Girraween, I couldn't help but feel that this suburb doesn't exactly roll out the welcome mat for a visitor looking for sights to see. To be blunt, there's not much on offer beyond endless houses neatly packed into tidy streets — a classic Sydney dormitory suburb. It's the sort of place that feels designed for people who need a place to sleep between battling traffic on the M4 and jumping on the train to work.

But here's where it gets interesting — my curiosity was piqued when I discovered that Girraween once formed part of the vast holdings of one D'Arcy Wentworth. Now *he* sounds like the sort of bloke who would've livened the place up.

D'Arcy was an Irishman from Portadown, County Armagh, and let's just say his path to Australia wasn't exactly smooth. He was acquitted of three charges of highway robbery back home — though he apparently dodged a fourth by volunteering to come to Botany Bay as an assistant surgeon in 1790.

Some might call that escaping justice; D'Arcy probably called it a fresh start.

Once here, he made quite the name for himself. By 1816 he was a mover and shaker in the colony, helping establish the Bank of New South Wales (which eventually became Westpac) and playing a key role in setting up the "Rum Hospital" — a place where payment for building the hospital was literally made in rum. When he died in 1827, D'Arcy was the wealthiest man in the colony, sitting on an impressive pile of land and cash, including some 22,000 acres — Girraween among them.

As for the name, Girraween supposedly means *"place of flowers"* in the local Aboriginal language. These days though, you'd be hard-pressed to find much floral abundance — maybe a few hardy roses in a front yard or two, but that's about it!

Fun Fact

The "Rum Hospital" D'Arcy Wentworth helped establish was so named because its builders were paid not in pounds but in rum — truly the spirit of early colonial enterprise!

Must See

- If you're driving through Girraween, this is more of a place to note the history than find a tourist highlight. If you're keen, nearby areas like Parramatta offer more for the visitor.

Key Statistics

- Location: Western Sydney, approx. 30 km from the Sydney CBD
- Population: Around 5,600
- Known for: Residential suburb, former estate of D'Arcy Wentworth
- Name origin: Aboriginal, thought to mean *"place of flowers"*

CHAPTER 52
BOGGABRI (NSW)

Well, it took me a while to actually find Boggabri. On a previous trip through the region, I somehow managed to completely miss it — no idea how! Maybe it was Boggabri's history of moving around that caught me out (that's my excuse, anyway). The original township, founded on the banks of the Namoi River, was swept away by floods in the 1850s. The town simply packed up and moved 20 kilometres north to higher, safer ground — and today it proudly claims to be the only Namoi River town that doesn't flood.

When I arrived, Boggabri was looking flat. I don't mean boring — I mean literally flat. No hills to speak of, which makes it easy to get your bearings. The town's a modest, quiet place of about 875 people, a small shopping strip, some tidy homes, and many locals working in the cotton industry.

The spot I was really keen to visit was Gins Leap, about 5 km north of town — but before we get there, let me detour into a rather tragic story connected to the area.

Back in October 1866, a woman named Maria Russell was tending to bulk spirits at an inn in Mungindi, a good 270 km north of here. A slush lamp's flame ignited the spirits, and the resulting blaze killed Maria and her young son, John James. Word of this disaster travelled south and eventually reached the Rock Inn — a pub and coach stop that once stood right at the foot of Gins Leap. The landlord and landlady of the Rock Inn, Mr and Mrs Glover, were Maria's parents.

On hearing the heartbreaking news, a horse team was dispatched to meet the coach carrying the bodies back to Boggabri. Maria, her child, and eventually Mr and Mrs Glover themselves were all buried near the Rock Inn, forming a poignant family plot. Their resting place was formalised in 1895 when a Danish tradesman, Christy Hansen, built a vault at the site. Also buried there is Mary Ann Mein, a 19-year-old who worked at the Rock Inn and died back in 1858. Her grave was moved during roadworks but her headstone now sits respectfully near the vault.

As for Gins Leap itself — well, like most evocative Aussie place names, there's a story behind it. Legend has it that a young Aboriginal girl, promised to an elder of the Kamilaroi people, ran away with a young man from another tribe. Pursued by Kamilaroi warriors, the pair reached the top of the rocky outcrop. Rather than be captured, they leapt to their deaths — and so, Gins Leap was named.

It's these kinds of stories that make places like Boggabri more than just dots on the map. I'm glad I made the effort to track it down at last — but now it's time to point the bonnet north again, towards Emmaville.

. . .

Fun Fact

Boggabri's claim to fame is being the only town on the Namoi River that *doesn't* flood — thanks to its relocation over 150 years ago!

Must See

- Gins Leap — a striking rock formation with a tragic love story attached.
- Historic cemetery at the foot of Gins Leap — graves of the Glover family and Mary Ann Mein.
- Boggabri town centre — a classic small-town stop with friendly locals.

Key Statistics

- Population: ~875
- Location: ~40 km north-west of Gunnedah
- Industry: Cotton and agriculture
- Elevation: approx. 240 metres

CHAPTER 53
EMMAVILLE (NSW)

After a night's stopover in Barrabri, I pushed on north towards Emmaville. Unfortunately, the weather gods weren't being kind — the rain got heavier, the skies darker, and by the time I tuned into the news, they were talking about towns being evacuated due to the worst flooding since 1990. So much for Queensland's pleasant autumn weather!

Luckily, my route kept me away from the worst-hit areas like Charleville and Roma — but it didn't steer me clear of Panther Country. Yes, you read that right: panthers.

Now, Australia is blessed with all manner of unique native wildlife — kangaroos, emus, koalas, wombats — but panthers aren't officially on that list. Unless, that is, you're talking to locals around Emmaville, who've been reporting panther sightings for well over a century.

The first reported encounter appeared in the *Inverell Times* back in 1902. A couple of blokes, Harry Leader and his brother, were camping out at Horse Stealers Gully, east of Keera, when they heard an unearthly roar. They caught sight of a creature in the firelight and, in true Aussie bush fashion, one of them shot it. They sent the animal off to Sydney for tanning, where the tanner supposedly confirmed it was — incredibly — a panther.

Fast forward half a century, and the sightings resumed. In 1958, locals started spotting big cats again. In the 1960s, sheep began turning up dead — reportedly up to 40 in a single weekend — with claw marks on their carcasses. The legend of the Emmaville Panther was well and truly alive.

But mythical beasts aside, Emmaville itself has an interesting history. It began as an agricultural outpost — Strathbogie Station — until tin was discovered here in 1872. The mining boom transformed the area, and the settlement became known as Vegetable Creek, thanks to the Chinese market gardens that sprang up to supply the miners.

At its peak around 1900, the town had a population of about 7,000 — around 2,000 of whom were Chinese. In 1882, the town was renamed Emmaville in honour of Lady Emma Loftus, wife of the then New South Wales Governor, Lord Augustus Loftus.

Curiously, the old name hasn't disappeared entirely — the local hospital is still called Vegetable Creek Hospital, keeping that quirky bit of history alive.

Fun Fact:

Emmaville is often considered Australia's unofficial "panther capital" — with alleged sightings continuing into the 21st century, sparking local debates and more than a few tall tales at the pub.

Must See:

- Emmaville Mining Museum — dedicated to the town's rich tin mining history
- 'Panther Country' sign — a great photo op for the believers
- Vegetable Creek Hospital building — with its links to the town's past
- Emmaville's charming streetscapes and country pubs

Key Statistics:

- Population: Approx. 300 today
- Location: New England region, northern New South Wales
- Elevation: Around 900 metres above sea level
- Known for: Tin mining heritage and the legendary Emmaville Panther

CHAPTER 54
WALLANGARRA (QLD)

I arrived in Wallangarra on a wet afternoon, the sort of rain that seems determined to get into your socks no matter what you do. As I pulled up, something caught my eye: a tree — yes, a tree — taking shelter under a shiny new tin shed. Curious, and in need of a bit of cover myself, I wandered over to investigate.

I'm starting to get used to this Aussie habit of preserving trees for prosperity — or posterity, depending on who you ask. These significant trees generally fall into two types. There are the famous "Black Stumps" that mark the symbolic start of the true outback — a kind of unofficial line where the settled country gives way to the wild — and then there are trees that were used as boundary markers back in the day.

This Wallangarra tree was one of the latter. It turns out it was the original survey marker when the border between New South Wales and Queensland was defined back in 1865. So there it stood, stoic and historical, enjoying its corrugated iron shelter like a dignified old gentleman in a raincoat.

Right next to this important bit of arboreal history was the Hotel Wallangarra — a pub with a cracking sense of humour. If you're coming from New South Wales, it proudly declares itself "The First Pub in Queensland," while for those heading the other way it's "The Last Pub in Queensland." Either way, it seems to be saying: *"Mate, stop in for a beer while you sort out what state you're in."*

When I visit these little towns, I always wonder: why does this place even exist? Most owe their origins to gold, tin, sheep or cattle — but Wallangarra's story is different. This town was built because of the railway... and one of Australia's classic transport blunders: the break-of-gauge.

Back in the day, nobody bothered coordinating rail networks between states. Queensland went with narrow gauge; New South Wales chose standard gauge. So when the two lines finally met here at Wallangarra, they didn't actually meet — at least, not in a convenient way. Everything — passengers, luggage, freight — had to be unloaded and reloaded at the border. It made Wallangarra an important, if awkward, cog in Australia's travel and trade network.

This little border town remained a vital link until 1932, when a standard gauge track was finally completed further east, making the whole break-of-gauge issue a bit of a relic. Scheduled rail services at Wallangarra finally stopped altogether in 1997, but the grand old station still stands — now as a museum — and the only train you'll see today is the static one parked out front.

With the rain easing off, I bid farewell to my sheltered tree companion, made a dash for the car, and set my sights on the next stop: Dalveen, further into Queensland.

. . .

Fun Fact:

Wallangarra's break-of-gauge station once featured platforms with different heights to accommodate the different trains from each state — the Queensland side lower than the New South Wales side!

Must See:

- The Wallangarra Railway Station Museum
- The border survey marker tree
- The "First/Last Pub in Queensland" for a cheeky photo opportunity and a cold one

Key statistics:

- Location: Border of NSW and Queensland
- Population: Approx. 385
- Altitude: 877 metres — making it one of Queensland's highest towns

CHAPTER 55
DALVEEN (QLD)

The rain was still falling steadily as I turned off the main road and into *Dalveen* — a tiny village that now sits quietly to the side thanks to the highway bypass. What I found was a classic one-street affair: a village store, a few houses, and not too much else to report.

Dalveen sits at the northern end of Queensland's *Granite Belt* — an area where the Great Dividing Range is made up of striking granite outcrops. The Great Dividing Range itself stretches over 3,500 km, but here the landscape is dominated by these boulders and rolling hills. At an altitude between 450m and 900m, this is the coolest part of Queensland — which may explain why, even in this sunny state, I found myself turning up the heater in the car!

The cooler climate also makes the region perfect for apple orchards — over a million apple trees spread across 55 orchards — and grapes for wine production. So while Dalveen itself doesn't have a whole lot going on, the surrounding district quietly underpins Queensland's apple and wine industries.

But on this visit? The rain, the mist, and the general chill meant that poor old Dalveen wasn't exactly shining as a tourist drawcard. After a quick look around and a nod to the village store, I decided to turn the heater up further and point the car south — back into New South Wales and onward to *Woodenbong*.

Fun Fact:

The Granite Belt is home to over a million apple trees — so even though Dalveen is tiny, the area punches well above its weight when it comes to apple production.

Must See:

- Dalveen village store
- Granite Belt scenery (best enjoyed on a fine day!)
- Nearby apple orchards and vineyards (bring an esky for fresh produce and wine)

Key statistics:

- Population: approx. 200
- Location: Northern end of Queensland's Granite Belt, about 25 km north of Stanthorpe
- Known for: granite outcrops, cool climate, apple orchards and vineyards

CHAPTER 56
WOODENBONG (NSW)

Leaving Dalveen, I crossed back into New South Wales — no grand border gate, just a modest sign — and took the turnoff to Woodenbong.

Now, there are rough roads... and then there's the road to Woodenbong. Technically sealed, but you wouldn't know it: bumps, twists and dips galore made the 30 km drive feel twice as long.

Eventually I rolled into this tiny village and was amused to find three places to refuel — quite the choice for a little country town. I went with the one sporting a classic Aussie touch: a veranda over the petrol pumps.

With all the rain, the town's Aboriginal name — said to mean "ducks on a lagoon" — felt perfectly appropriate. But I wasn't here for ducks... I was here for something far more elusive: the Yowie.

While the Himalayas have the Yeti and North America has Bigfoot, Australia has the Yowie — and Woodenbong proudly claims to be one of its stomping grounds. Sightings go back decades, including reports of short, hairy creatures with long arms and heads sunk into their shoulders, and a more recent account of a tall ape-like figure vanishing into the mist.

Sadly, there was no Yowie waiting to greet me at the petrol pumps — just the regular *Woodenbong Yowie Country Market* keeping the legend alive. If you're keen to spot one, that might be your best bet... though I reckon you'll have better luck finding ducks.

Fun Fact:

Woodenbong's Aboriginal name means *"ducks on a lagoon"* — but it's also known among cryptozoologists as *prime Yowie country*.

Must See:

- Woodenbong petrol stations (there are surprisingly many!)
- The road into town — a test of any suspension system
- Keep an eye out for Yowies... just in case

Key statistics:

- Population: approx. 400
- Location: Northern NSW, near the QLD border
- Known for: bumpy roads, peaceful scenery... and Yowie legends

CHAPTER 57
TOOWOOMBA (QLD)

I rolled into *Toowoomba* late in the day, with the rain still falling and the sky already darkening. But even in this soggy state, the town's nickname — *"The Garden City"* — felt appropriate. The place practically glowed green, with the recent rains encouraging every leaf, blade of grass and flower to burst into colour.

I had two missions in Toowoomba. First, I needed an umbrella. With all this rain, I figured the surest way to stop it was to buy one — and true to form, once I did, the downpours eased off, replaced by the occasional light shower. I'd like to think my purchase saved one or two locals from getting flooded out that day.

My second mission was more pressing, at least for me: finally solving the mystery of *Cobb and Co.*

Now, to many Aussies, this probably isn't a mystery at all. But as a *Pom*, I'd long wondered what exactly Cobb and Co was — it pops up everywhere: Cobb and Co inns, staging posts, plaques... but what *was* it?

Thankfully, *Toowoomba* is home to the *Cobb & Co Museum* so I figured this was my chance to put that curiosity to rest.

After admiring an impressive outdoor display of old windmills, I made sure I was at the museum right on opening at 10am. The friendly assistant took my entry fee (politely pointing out that it would have been free if I was a Toowoomba resident — a nice local perk) and sent me off to explore.

Now I have to confess... horse-drawn carriages have never really been my thing. Let's be honest: they're pretty basic contraptions — a seat, a few wheels and somewhere to attach the poor beast expected to pull it.

But the Cobb & Co Museum doesn't hold back: they have every kind of carriage you can imagine. Tiny buggies for one, grand coaches for many, wagons for timber, even carriages pulled by goats and dogs!

Amongst all this, there were also excellent displays on Toowoomba's history, local Aboriginal culture and wildlife. And, of course, a decent coffee shop — essential for any serious museum-goer.

But I was here for Cobb and Co, and happily I found what I was looking for: three original Cobb and Co coaches on display — Coach numbers 48, 100 and 112.

So, what did I learn?

Cobb and Co began back in 1853 when three Americans, led by Freeman Cobb, decided to set up a stagecoach service in Victoria. Originally called the "American Telegraph Line of Coaches" (not exactly catchy), it quickly got abbreviated in true Aussie fashion to *Cobb and Co*.

The service worked in "stages" — horses and coaches covering 25–40 km at a time before fresh teams took over. The first journey was on 20 January 1854 between Melbourne and Castlemaine.

By the 1860s, Cobb and Co was expanding fast — into New South Wales in 1865 and Queensland in 1866. But its decline started in the 1890s as railways and motor vehicles took over.

The last Cobb and Co coach ran on 14 August 1924 between *Yuleba* and *Surat*. After that, it was all downhill. Even though Cobb and Co tried using motor vehicles, the Great Depression sealed its fate and the company went into voluntary liquidation in 1929.

It's incredible, though — no matter where you travel in Australia, some connection to Cobb and Co pops up. From staging posts and coach factories to breeding studs for coach horses, this business was once the literal backbone of transport in the bush.

Thanks to Toowoomba's excellent museum, I can now say I understand the legend of Cobb and Co a little better — and I'm glad I made the stop.

Fun Fact:

The Cobb and Co service started as the "American Telegraph Line of Coaches" but, in classic Aussie style, the name got shortened almost immediately — because who has time for all those words?

Must See:

- *Cobb & Co Museum* — even if you're not mad about carriages, it's well worth it
- The windmill display outside the museum
- Toowoomba's lush gardens (even in the rain!)

Key statistics:

- Population: approx. 137,000
- Location: Southern Queensland, west of Brisbane
- Known for: "The Garden City", Cobb & Co connections, annual Toowoomba Carnival of Flowers

CHAPTER 58
NAMBOUR (QLD)

On the outskirts of Nambour, in the little town of Woombye, I was delighted to stumble across my second "Big" Australian icon of this journey — The Big Pineapple!

I sat in the car for a few minutes, just marvelling at this 16-metre-high fibreglass spectacle. It's genuinely impressive — easily qualifying for the mythical Australian Hall of Big Things (surely we must have one by now?).

As I watched, a steady stream of tourists did the classic Aussie "Big Thing" routine: stop the car, jump out, snap a photo, then straight back in and off down the road. A few adventurous souls actually wandered into the restaurant and gift shop that proudly advertised "Free Admission" — a tempting proposition for those easily swayed by stuffed kangaroos, mixed preserves, and novelty tea towels.

The Big Pineapple was unveiled back on 15 August 1971, originally accompanied by a 56-acre pineapple plantation (later expanded to a whopping 113 hectares). Like many Aussie icons, it's had a colourful history.

In 1978, the adjoining fruit market and restaurant burned down but rose again phoenix-like — this time with a Macadamia Factory and the now-legendary Nutmobile Tour! Ownership changed hands several times, including a stint under Rupert Murdoch's Queensland Newspapers (who knew Rupert was into giant fruit?) before being sold again in 1996.

When I ventured inside the shop, I meandered past the stuffed animals and jars of preserves before landing at the cafeteria where I enjoyed a coffee and cake on the veranda. From there, I gazed out over the plantation below as the heavens opened and the rain began bucketing down — a fitting Queensland scene if ever there was one.

With the rain pouring, I gave the Nutmobile a miss (a decision I stand by), but I did learn an odd little fact: once upon a time, there were actually two Big Pineapples in Queensland.

The second one stood proudly at Gympie, just 65 kilometres away, opened barely two months later — on 15 October 1971 for Gympie's 104th birthday — and almost identical in height. There's long been a playful rivalry between the two towns about who built it first, with whispers of shared plans and friendly one-upmanship.

Whatever the story, Gympie's pineapple came down in 2008... which means the Woombye pineapple reigns supreme today as Queensland's last Big Pineapple standing.

Fun Fact:

At one point, there were two almost identical Big Pineapples in Queensland — Woombye's opened in August 1971, Gympie's in October 1971 — sparking a mini "pineapple rivalry".

Must See:

- The Big Pineapple itself — 16 metres of fibreglass fruit glory
- The café and veranda for a classic "cuppa with a view"
- The pineapple plantation stretching out below

Key statistics:

- Location: Woombye, Sunshine Coast hinterland
- Height: 16 metres
- Known for: Being an iconic "Big Thing" and home to the legendary Nutmobile

CHAPTER 59
MAROOCHYDORE (QLD)

Maroochydore was quiet when I arrived... and just as quiet when I left. The weather was to blame — drizzle and grey skies keeping holiday-makers away. Had the sun been shining, I'm sure the place would have been buzzing, with its beaches full and the resort-town energy on full display.

Instead, I wandered almost alone through a damp beachside park, past a few youths sheltering from the rain under a barbecue shelter, and took in the view of the sea — grey, but still beautiful.

The *Maroochy River* is a defining feature here, flowing gently beside the town which sits on its southern bank. These days, *Sunshine Plaza* — the Sunshine Coast's largest shopping centre — is the modern hub, while tall apartment blocks line the coast. Yet despite the obvious development, the surf beaches remain the town's beating heart.

Standing there by the shore, I couldn't help recalling a

striking incident from Maroochydore's past — one of those tragic stories that sticks in your mind.

It was 11am on 30 December 1950. Picture the scene: a classic Aussie summer's day. Crystal-clear water, blue skies, golden sand lined with 1,000 people enjoying the height of the season. Overhead, an Australian Air Force Wirraway aircraft was performing shark patrol duties — a common sight in those days.

But something went horribly wrong.

As the plane dipped lower for a closer look at a suspected shark near the breakers, it accidentally touched the water, lost control and crashed straight onto the packed beach. The aftermath was devastating: beach umbrellas and belongings scattered across the sand, three young children killed and 14 others injured. A day that should have been filled with sunshine and laughter instead became a tragic chapter in the town's history. That tragedy still casts a shadow over the local memory, even as today's beach feels tranquil and carefree.

Thankfully, some 60 years on, tranquility was all I found here — especially on this damp, sleepy day in March. So, after a contemplative stroll, I headed back to the car and pointed it just a little further south... next stop: *Mooloolaba*.

Fun Fact:

The name *Maroochydore* is derived from the Yuggera language word *"Muru-kutchi"*, meaning "red-bill" — a reference to the black swans that once flourished here.

Must See:

- Maroochydore Beach and Cotton Tree parklands
- Maroochy River views
- Sunshine Plaza for a browse
- Surf beaches that stretch as far as the eye can see

Key statistics:

- Population: approx. 17,000
- Location: Sunshine Coast, Queensland
- Known for: beaches, the Maroochy River, Sunshine Plaza, laid-back coastal vibe

CHAPTER 60
MOOLOOLABA (QLD)

The *Mooloolaba* tourism website says it all, really:

"Welcome to sun-kissed beaches, boutique shopping and atmospheric dining – in Mooloolaba. Come as you are."

And it feels exactly like that. To me, Mooloolaba comes across as a slightly more polished, boutique version of neighbouring *Maroochydore* — a "mini-me" that's just that little bit more exclusive, sophisticated and stylish. No doubt the prices of accommodation reflect this too!

It's a breezy, laid-back place — but with an upmarket edge. Designer boutiques, waterfront cafés and pristine beaches all invite you to slow down and soak it in.

One of the standout landmarks in town is an imposing statue of none other than *Steve Irwin*, the Crocodile Hunter himself. Given his deep ties to the Sunshine Coast — after all, Australia Zoo is just up the road — the locals were determined to honour him.

Mayor Joe Natoli personally approached the Irwin family for their blessing, which they gave wholeheartedly. Terri Irwin told the *Sunshine Coast Daily*:

"Steve was a fair-dinkum Australian who was proud to call the Sunshine Coast home. Bindi, Robert and I would like to thank Joe Natoli and everyone in this area for such an amazing tribute."

There's a lesser-known bit of Steve Irwin trivia too: between 1980 and 1984, he worked for the local council as an apprentice diesel fitter at the Nambour Depot. In typical Steve style, when he left the job, he left his mark — literally. He grabbed a can of grease and scrawled "Yahoo" on a depot wall. It's still there today, a small but classic piece of Crocodile Hunter graffiti.

After a wander along the beach, past designer shops and the statue of one of Australia's most iconic larrikins, I couldn't help but think: yep, *Mooloolaba really does invite you to "come as you are"... as long as you've got a few extra dollars in your pocket.*

Fun Fact:

Steve Irwin worked for the Sunshine Coast Council in the early 1980s and left behind his own bit of "local heritage" — a "Yahoo" graffitied wall at the Nambour Depot that's still there today.

Must See:

- Mooloolaba Beach — one of the Sunshine Coast's finest

- Steve Irwin statue — a fitting tribute to the Crocodile Hunter
- Boutique shops and waterfront cafés along the esplanade

Key statistics:

- Population: approx. 7,000
- Location: Sunshine Coast, Queensland
- Known for: beaches, boutique shopping, upmarket coastal vibe, Crocodile Hunter connection

CHAPTER 61
STRATHPINE (QLD)

I left Mooloolaba early, keen to avoid the Brisbane traffic... which of course meant I arrived in Strathpine bang on cue for the morning rush hour. Perfect timing, right? This north-side suburb, unlike the beach charms of Mooloolaba or Maroochydore, isn't about sand and surf — it's about practicality. Gympie Road slices through, busy with commuters, flanked by shopping centres that cater to the locals going about their daily lives.

Strathpine didn't exactly spring up for its beauty, but rather thanks to fortune and sugar. When gold was discovered at Gympie in 1867, people started pouring through here, and the railway soon followed — lending the place its name. By the 1870s, Strathpine was a hive of industry with three sugar mills cranking away. Only one was destined to last, reinventing itself as the *Normanby Distillery*, famous for knocking out barrels of quality rum — over 5,000 litres a day at its peak.

Sadly, the distillery called last drinks in 1968, but not before one final hurrah that could only happen in Queensland: vandals broke in, cracked open the vats, and 7,500 litres of maturing rum flowed into the South Pine River. I'm sure the fish didn't mind, though I doubt they swam straight after that.

The Bennett family, who ran the distillery from 1908 for around fifty years, saw the business taken over by Queensland United Foods before the building was eventually demolished in 1975. In a poetic twist, one of the Bennett family members went searching for any remaining stock. The trail led him to a pub in Gympie, where he found what was believed to be the very last bottle of Normanby rum. That's dedication — and possibly a very expensive round.

Fun Fact:

Strathpine is the only place in Queensland where a rum distillery's final act involved turning the local river into an impromptu cocktail.

Must See:

- *Pine Rivers Heritage Museum* — a great spot for those curious about Strathpine's sugar and rum-soaked past.
- *South Pine River Parklands* — not far from where all that rum once flowed!

Key Statistics:

- Population: Approx. 9,500
- Location: About 20 km north of Brisbane CBD
- Claim to fame: Once home to Normanby Rum, a Queensland icon

CHAPTER 62
INDOOROOPILLY (QLD)

Indooroopilly — like *Strathpine* before it — is another Brisbane suburb that's mainly residential, dominated by a large shopping centre (this time the biggest in Brisbane's western suburbs) and plenty of traffic.

I popped into the shopping centre... but promptly popped out again when I realised I'd forgotten my wallet. So much for retail therapy.

As for the name *Indooroopilly*, there's a bit of debate about its meaning. It may come from *Yindurupilli*, meaning "gully of running water", or *Nyindur-pilly*, meaning "gully of the leeches" — one rather more appealing than the other, depending on your perspective!

Now, here's something you probably wouldn't expect in a busy Brisbane suburb: *Indooroopilly has its own mine.* Yep, tucked away here is the *University of Queensland Experimental Mine*, with a history that goes back to 1918. Apparently, a bloke called P.J. Madden and his mate G. Olsen discovered a valuable bit of mineral in someone's garden rockery. Never let a good rock go to waste — they secured a mining lease and on 1 November 1918 started digging properly.

Their first haul — 12 tons of ore — went off to a smelter in NSW and yielded 1,245 ounces of silver and 8 tons of lead, netting them a tidy £282. Not bad for a rockery discovery!

But as is often the case, things didn't last. Two more mining attempts followed but were eventually defeated by a combination of falling mineral prices, rising wages and flooding. By 1929, mining at Indooroopilly was over.

The site later became Brisbane City Council property before the University of Queensland snapped it up in 1951 for its Department of Mining and Metallurgical Engineering. Today, it's still in use as a world-class research centre — the *Julius Kruttschnitt Mine Research Centre* — complete with an open pit and restored underground shafts.

Sadly, the mine isn't open to the public, so after learning about its fascinating history, I was back to the shopping centre for entertainment... and that didn't last long either. So I did what any sensible traveller would do — moved on to the next stop: *Yeerongpilly*.

Fun Fact:

The first silver-lead ore mined at Indooroopilly in 1918 came from a discovery in someone's backyard rockery!

Must See:

- Julius Kruttschnitt Mine Research Centre (you can't actually visit — but it's interesting to know it's there!)

- Indooroopilly Shopping Centre (especially if you remember your wallet)

Key statistics:

- Population: approx. 12,000
- Location: Brisbane's western suburbs
- Known for: massive shopping centre, traffic... and a secret university mine

CHAPTER 63
YEERONGPILLY (QLD)

Yeerongpilly — what a name. It rolls off the tongue in a delightfully Aussie way and, as it turns out, comes from the Aboriginal words "yarung" meaning sandy or gravelly (or possibly "yurong" meaning rain) and "pilly" meaning gully or watercourse. So basically, "rainy sandy gully" — which feels about right for Brisbane.

First impressions? Yeerongpilly is a bit of a mix. It's centred around a one-way system and a rather peculiar roundabout arrangement, giving the whole place a slightly disorienting feel. The suburb is immediately industrial in character — plenty of car repair shops, workshops and the like — and it's home to a large Asian community and a growing Sub-Saharan African population, giving it a distinct multicultural flavour.

Tourist attractions? Honestly, there aren't any. Yeerongpilly doesn't pretend to be a tourist town.

After a bit of wandering through the industrial hub, I veered off into a quiet residential street where life felt much slower.

Here, there were just a few modest houses, a small kids' playground... and, unexpectedly, the entrance to Brisbane Golf Club.

Founded in 1896 and located at Yeerongpilly since 1903, Brisbane Golf Club is Queensland's first full-length course — an impressive slice of golfing history quietly tucked away in this unassuming suburb.

After a quick look around, I realised there wasn't much else to detain me — no cafés begging for custom, no quirky shops or historical plaques — just a straightforward, workaday suburb going about its business. Sometimes that's all you need to tick a place off the list.

Fun Fact:

Brisbane Golf Club, hidden here in Yeerongpilly, was Queensland's very first full-length golf course — founded in 1896 and still going strong.

Must See:

- Brisbane Golf Club for a slice of sporting history
- Quiet residential streets — perfect for a peaceful wander
- The peculiar one-way system and roundabout arrangement (best appreciated from behind the wheel)

Key statistics:

- Population: approx. 2,000

- Location: Brisbane's southside, about 7 km from the CBD
- Known for: industrial vibe, multicultural population, Brisbane Golf Club

CHAPTER 64
COOLANGATTA (QLD)

Rolling into Coolangatta, I couldn't shake the feeling I'd been here before. Long stretches of golden sand, towering apartment blocks casting shadows over boutique shops and surf stores — it all felt a bit familiar. Truth be told, it's got a lot in common with other big-name surf spots along the Aussie coast.

In fact, it reminded me a little of Collaroy down in Sydney, and here's a curious coincidence: just like Collaroy, Coolangatta got its name from a shipwreck.

Back in 1846, the *Coolangatta* — an 83-foot schooner — was caught in a wild storm and wrecked right here. Miraculously, no lives were lost. The survivors legged it 70 miles north to Amity Point, taking six days to make the journey, and were looked after along the way by generous local Indigenous groups. I reckon that's a pretty decent walk — and probably not the sort of stroll you'd fancy after your boat's come to grief.

But it wasn't until 1884 that the name *Coolangatta* was officially pinned to this place, thanks to Henry Schneider, a government surveyor who clearly thought naming towns after shipwrecks was the done thing.

These days, Coolangatta is classic surf-town material: sun, sand, salty air and the laid-back vibe to match. It's the sort of place where your thongs double as formal wear and nobody's in too much of a hurry — except maybe for the next decent set rolling in.

Fun Fact:

The name *Coolangatta* comes from an Aboriginal word meaning "splendid view" — very appropriate given the outlook from just about anywhere along the beach.

Must See:

- Snapper Rocks — a mecca for surfers chasing world-class waves.
- Coolangatta Beach itself — golden sand and plenty of room to stretch out.
- Point Danger Lookout — for cracking coastal views and a handy monument marking the NSW/QLD border.

Key statistics:

- Population: Around 6,000
- Location: Southernmost suburb of the Gold Coast, right on the Queensland-NSW border

- Claim to fame: Legendary surf breaks and relaxed beach culture

CHAPTER 65
TAMBORINE (QLD)

There are several Queensland towns that carry the name *Tamborine*: *Mount Tamborine*, *North Tamborine*... and my destination today, the plain and simple *Tamborine*. No frills, no extras — just *Tamborine*.

The main junction into town, where a small cluster of stores sit, gives you a fair sense of the place. Beyond that, the rest of the village is a scattering of well-spaced homes, dotted among woodlands and open pastures. It has a quiet, almost sleepy feel to it — peaceful and pleasant but definitely a "blink and you'll miss it" kind of place.

I must admit, my research didn't turn up any thrilling historical tales or quirky trivia to share about *Tamborine*. In fact, the only notable fact I stumbled across was that a 47-year-old woman had to be airlifted to Royal Brisbane Hospital after a horse fell on her here back in January 2009. Hardly the stuff of travel brochures!

But sometimes that's the charm of these smaller places —

there's not much to *do* but simply appreciate the quiet, rural atmosphere.

So after a quick wander and a pause to take in the surrounds, I was ready to move on to the next stop — but glad to have ticked another name off the list.

Fun Fact:

Despite sharing the name, *Tamborine* itself is quite distinct from the better-known *Mount Tamborine* up the road — smaller, quieter and even more rural.

Must See:

- The peaceful country roads and pastures around Tamborine
- The village centre — small but welcoming

Key statistics:

- Population: approx. 3,900
- Location: Scenic Rim region, southeast Queensland
- Known for: rural lifestyle, proximity to Tamborine Mountain and surrounding natural beauty

CHAPTER 66
FINGAL (QLD)

If you type Fingal into Google Maps, chances are it'll send you straight to Fingal in Tasmania — but that's not the Fingal Geoff Mack had in mind when he wrote I've Been Everywhere. I know this for a fact, because I asked him! Geoff told me that the Fingal he was thinking of when penning the song was Fingal Head in New South Wales — so naturally, that's where I pointed the car.

It's worth noting that, aside from Darwin, all of Geoff's locations fall into just three Australian states: Queensland, Victoria, and New South Wales. Why? Simple: when Geoff wrote the song, he was sitting in his panel van with maps of only those three states — so they're what made the cut!

Fingal Head sits just south of the Queensland border on the southern side of the Tweed River. It's a quiet, sleepy little coastal settlement — home to around 600 people, although as I drove around, the only locals I spotted were a handful of fishermen trying their luck.

The highlight here is the Fingal Head Lighthouse, originally built in 1878. It's a classic little lighthouse perched on the headland, and from the cliffs nearby you can look out over the ocean to see a striking rock formation called the Giant's Causeway. These basalt columns look remarkably similar to their famous namesake in Northern Ireland — and depending on which source you believe, they're either named after that Irish site or after Fingal's Cave on the Scottish island of Staffa.

Either way, it's an impressive natural feature — a reminder that even tucked-away spots like Fingal Head can hold surprises for those who venture off the beaten track.

Fun Fact:

Geoff Mack wrote *I've Been Everywhere* using maps he happened to have in his panel van at the time — meaning most of his towns, including Fingal, came from Queensland, Victoria and New South Wales!

Must See:

- Fingal Head Lighthouse (1878)
- Giant's Causeway basalt columns
- Scenic views over the Tweed coast

Key statistics:

- Population: approx. 600
- Location: Tweed Coast, NSW, just south of the QLD border

- Known for: lighthouse, basalt rock formations, peaceful seaside vibe

CHAPTER 67
MURWILLUMBAH (QLD)

The drive into Murwillumbah is nothing short of spectacular. Mount Warning (or Wollumbin, as it's known to the Bundjalung people) rises dramatically in the distance, surrounded by lush, rolling green countryside. The hills are dotted with sugar cane fields and banana plantations — clearly this is fertile land, and it shows.

The town itself looks to be doing just fine too. I parked near the local RSL Club and set off for a wander around the streets.

You wouldn't know it by looking today, but Murwillumbah has had its fair share of knocks: a devastating fire in 1907 that destroyed much of the town, numerous major floods over the years, and Australia's largest — and still unsolved — bank robbery in 1978, when $1,763,000 vanished without a trace.

Yet here it is, standing proud, bustling with life and seemingly thriving. The townsfolk — which now include a fair few seachangees who've swapped city life for this Northern Rivers haven — seem to be prospering just fine.

There's a warm, welcoming vibe here, and plenty of little shops and cafés worth a browse — all framed by that ever-present backdrop of Wollumbin.

Fun Fact:

In 1978, Murwillumbah was the scene of Australia's largest and still-unsolved bank robbery, when $1,763,000 disappeared from the vault of the local bank!

Must See:

- Murwillumbah's main street and shops
- Views of Mount Warning / Wollumbin
- Murwillumbah RSL Club — classic country-town gathering place

Key statistics:

- Population: approx. 9,200
- Location: Northern Rivers, NSW, near the Queensland border
- Known for: fertile farmland, rich history, resilient community, proximity to Mount Warning

CHAPTER 68
MULLUMBIMBY (QLD)

Mullumbimby is just 4 km off the Pacific Highway... but it could easily feel like 1,000 km. The moment you turn off the highway, the pace drops, the noise fades, and you find yourself in a peaceful country town that serves as a real hub for the surrounding farms and hinterland communities.

As I wandered through, I was struck by how serene it all felt — a far cry from the bustling vibe of nearby Byron Bay. What I didn't realise at the time was that back in the late 1960s, Mullumbimby was one of Australia's great alternative lifestyle centres. It was a magnet for the counterculture movement — right up there with Nimbin and Byron Bay.

But unlike those neighbours, Mullumbimby doesn't really flaunt that history today. There are no tie-dye shops on every corner, no crystal emporiums or psychedelic murals. You'd be hard-pressed to find much that overtly celebrates that chapter of its past.

Maybe all those old Mullumbimby hippies have traded in their kombis and are now chilling out quietly at the local bowls club? Who knows — but there's still an easygoing, welcoming air about the place.

Fun Fact:

In the 1960s and '70s, Mullumbimby was one of Australia's counterculture hotspots — but today it's kept things understated, unlike its famous neighbour Byron Bay.

Must See:

- The peaceful town centre
- Local shops and cafés that reflect Mullum's laid-back character
- Hinterland views as you drive in and out of town

Key statistics:

- Population: approx. 3,600
- Location: Northern Rivers, NSW — 20 km north of Byron Bay
- Known for: relaxed country-town vibe, alternative lifestyle roots, community spirit

CHAPTER 69
BANGALOW (NSW)

Just inland from Australia's most easterly point, Byron Bay, is Bangalow — a cracking little spot that feels like the perfect place to while away a lazy Sunday. It's the sort of town where you half expect to bump into Miss Marple popping out of a tearoom, such is its charming, 'olde worlde' feel.

Walking down the high street here is a bit like stepping back in time. No high-rises, no hustle — just a single main street lined with quaint shops and historic buildings, all nestled snugly amongst rolling green hills that wouldn't look out of place in the English Home Counties.

Presiding over it all is the Catholic Church of St Kevin, keeping a quiet watch over the comings and goings of this sleepy but delightful town.

Fun Fact:

The name 'Bangalow' comes from the Aboriginal word *'Bangalla'*, meaning "a low hill" or "a kind of palm tree" — quite fitting really, given the town's lush surrounds.

Must See:

- The beautifully preserved Federation-style shopfronts
- Bangalow Heritage House Museum & Tea Rooms
- The monthly Bangalow Markets (a treasure trove for arts, crafts, and produce)
- St Kevin's Catholic Church for a peaceful moment and cracking views over town

Key Statistics:

- Population: Around 2,000
- Location: Approximately 15km inland from Byron Bay, NSW
- Known for: Federation architecture, artisan shops, community markets, and a relaxed village atmosphere

CHAPTER 70
LISMORE (NSW)

Lismore was my final destination for the day — and after squeezing in a few too many stops (the towns being so close together), I was glad to pull into town, quickly find a motel, and have a moment to relax before heading out for a wander.

First impressions? Lismore felt like a hive of activity — a proper regional hub, bustling with locals going about their business. But I couldn't help noticing that much of the town centre looked... well... a bit like a bomb site. Streets torn up, roadworks everywhere, and plenty of barriers and detours.

I'm sure it's not normally like this — I'd clearly arrived in the middle of a serious renovation blitz. A reminder that even country towns need a spruce-up from time to time.

Lismore has some interesting roots too. The town was named after Lismore in Scotland, thanks to Scottish settlers William and Jane Wilson. The Wilsons arrived in NSW in 1833 (not 1883 — one of those little historical mix-ups) and took up an abandoned sheep run in 1845. They chose the name after honeymooning on the Scottish Lismore, a romantic gesture that stuck and gave this bustling Northern Rivers town its name.

Today, Lismore is a key centre for the surrounding Northern Rivers region — a service town with a strong community spirit, plenty of cafes, galleries, and a reputation for alternative culture and creativity.

I didn't have as much time as I'd have liked to explore its charms this time, but even with roadworks everywhere, there was still an energy about the place. Next time, I'd like to dig a little deeper — after the dust settles.

Fun Fact:

Lismore is known as the "Rainbow Region" and has a thriving **arts and alternative lifestyle scene** — the Mardi-Grass festival at nearby Nimbin is just one example of its quirky local culture.

Must See:

- Lismore Regional Gallery — one of Australia's oldest regional galleries
- Heritage buildings around the CBD — charming, even with a few detours
- The Wilson River — named after that same pioneering family
- Local cafés — excellent coffee and eclectic atmosphere

Key Statistics:

- Population: Approx. 28,000
- Location: Northern Rivers, NSW
- Elevation: Around 12 metres above sea level
- Known for: Arts and culture, Scottish heritage, regional hub for surrounding farming communities

CHAPTER 71
CASINO (NSW)

You'd think a place called Casino would be flashing neon, poker machines jangling, maybe the odd punter staggering out at sunrise. But no — there's no casino here at all. Turns out the name came from the Italian town of Cassino, but somewhere along the line an Aussie bureaucrat must have had a long lunch and dropped an 's', leaving us with plain old *Casino*. Typical.

I rolled into town early, when most locals were still tucked up in bed — except for the cows, of course. And that's really what Casino is all about: cattle. The self-proclaimed Beef Capital of Australia. (Although if you ask anyone from Rockhampton, they'll tell you the same thing. I reckon there's enough beef to keep both towns happy.)

Casino's main streets were quiet, clean, and wide — very 'country town' vibes — but pretty empty at that hour. I didn't linger long in the centre; instead, I followed the road out past lush green paddocks where curious cattle looked up as I passed by, probably wondering who this bloke was disturbing their morning chew.

Fun Fact:

Casino once hosted a "Beef Capital" tug-of-war contest against Rockhampton... but nobody can quite agree who won!

Must See:

- Casino's annual Beef Week festival — if you want to experience this town in full swing, that's when to come.
- Richmond River and surrounding countryside — perfect for a scenic drive.
- Heritage buildings in Walker Street.

Key statistics:

- Location: Northern Rivers region, NSW
- Population: Around 11,000
- Known for: Beef cattle, rural charm, quiet mornings!

CHAPTER 72
DORRIGO (NSW)

Dorrigo is a little gem of a town. Not because it's hiding diamonds or opals — at least, not that I know of — but because it just feels different from a lot of places I'd been wandering through recently. It's just the right size: big enough to keep you interested, small enough to cover in a day. Just remember your brolly — this is officially the wettest town in New South Wales.

Driving in, I couldn't help stopping for a quick selfie at the town sign, and almost straight away I spotted railway carriages. First one, then another, and soon steam locomotives too — iron ghosts of another era scattered across paddocks.

Curiosity won, so I ducked down a few side streets and there it was: the Dorrigo Steam Railway and Museum, or at least the beginnings of it. A vast collection of preserved railway history — everything from ancient steam engines to rolling stock — quietly rusting away in the rain. The museum isn't open yet, though they've been working on it since 1973 and have raised over $7 million so far. It still looks like it's a while off. I stood there admiring this sea of rusting history just as the Google Street View car trundled past — somewhere out there, I reckon there's an image of me grinning madly next to a steam engine.

By now I was ready for breakfast. In town I found a delightful little bookshop-cum-café — two of my favourite things combined. After a browse and a bite, I spotted the *Don Dorrigo Gazette* on the counter. It looked so quaint I couldn't resist grabbing a copy. The Gazette really was a time capsule: black and white, no photos, all printed on an old-school letterpress.

In fact, the *Don Dorrigo Gazette* was famous for being the last newspaper in Australia — possibly the world — still printed on a letterpress. I was lucky enough to visit the tiny office tucked down a laneway. The publisher, Michael, kindly gave me a peek at the clattering machine, patiently churning out about a thousand copies a week. Slow, painstaking work, but with a charm no modern printer could match.

Sadly, I later learned that in 2023, the Gazette finally closed after more than a century in print — another little piece of history gone.

Before leaving, I made a last essential stop: Dangar Falls. Thanks to all the rain, they were absolutely roaring — the perfect, dramatic end to a visit to a town that quietly punches above its weight.

Fun Fact:

The Don Dorrigo Gazette, established in 1910, was the last

newspaper in Australia (and possibly the world) to be produced entirely on a hot-metal letterpress system.

Must See:

- Dorrigo Steam Railway and Museum (even if you can't go inside — it's worth peering over fences)
- Dangar Falls (especially after rain)
- Stroll through the lovely town centre — classic country town vibe with quirky little shops and cafés

Key Statistics:

- Population: Around 1,000
- Location: Mid North Coast hinterland, New South Wales
- Elevation: Approx. 750 metres above sea level — expect mist and drizzle!
- Known for: Rain, waterfalls, railway relics, and timeless charm

CHAPTER 73
TAREE (NSW)

I rolled into Taree one Friday arvo, just as the rain decided to make itself known. Perfect timing really — it gave me a chance to christen my brand-new umbrella while wandering the streets. The usual suspects were all here: familiar shops lining the main drag, and even a decent-sized shopping centre tucked away. It didn't take long to get a sense that Taree's no sleepy backwater — it's a proper regional hub.

But interestingly, it hasn't always been top dog in this part of the world. Back in the day, nearby Wingham was where all the action was, serving as the administrative centre. That all changed in 1913 when the railway chose Taree and snubbed Wingham, setting Taree up as the go-to town for business and trade.

Speaking of local claims to fame, Taree sits beside the Manning River — a mighty stretch of water that produces over three million oysters a year. To mark this slimy achievement, the town built itself a "Big Oyster" — because, as any Aussie knows, a proper town needs a "big" something to feel complete. Sadly, this particular attraction was less of a pearl and more of a dud. Locals fondly (or perhaps not so fondly) refer to it as the "Big Mistake". These days, it's a quirky home for a motor dealership — but if you're a fan of Australia's Big Things, it's worth a quick look.

For a bit of local language flavour, the town's name comes from the Biripi word "tareebit", meaning tree by the river — more specifically, the sandpaper fig, a native tree that lines the banks here.

Fun Fact:

The Big Oyster was built by the same crew responsible for Ballina's Big Prawn — clearly experts in all things oversized and fibreglass.

Must See:

- The Big Oyster (even if just for a photo and a chuckle)
- Manning River foreshore walk
- Manning Regional Art Gallery

Key statistics:

- Population: approx. 26,000
- Located on the banks of the Manning River
- Major industries: agriculture, aquaculture (especially oysters), and regional commerce

CHAPTER 74
STOCKINBINGAL (NSW)

Stockinbingal looks like it's seen happier times. As you drive into town, you can't help but notice the row of old shopfronts on one side of the street — once the bustling heart of this small village, now mostly closed up and silent. Only a couple still hang on: the village store and the Commercial Hotel.

The original hotel, built in 1892, was a stopover point for the Cobb & Co coaches travelling between Harden and Temora. Most of the other buildings look as though they've been kept going purely for prosperity's sake — preserved, but their doors firmly shut, and unlikely to open again anytime soon.

The town is home to just 244 people, and its origins are firmly tied to the railways. Stockinbingal is, according to Wikipedia, "the location of a railway junction connecting the Cootamundra to Lake Cargelligo line (completed in 1893) to Parkes, which provides an alternative route from Sydney to Parkes, avoiding the steep grades of the Blue Mountains. As a result, it's now the major route for freight between Sydney and Perth."

This junction is also part of a clever bypass route for rail traffic between Melbourne and Brisbane via Dubbo, Werris Creek and Maitland — making tiny Stockinbingal a surprisingly important cog in the national freight network.

As for the name? Like many Aussie towns, there's a bit of debate. Some say Stockinbingal means "full belly". Others suggest the name relates to the local water supply, now known as Bland Creek, which the local Aboriginal people called Tocumbidgie or Tocumbimbil. The words themselves have meanings like "deep hole" and "white-leafed box tree," but at some point along the way, the letters seem to have got rearranged — and we ended up with Stockinbingal.

There's not much here for the visitor these days, but if you pause to read the history on some of the buildings, it's fascinating. The old bakery, pictured here, opened in 1913 and served locals until 1968.

It's a classic story of a small town whose heyday is behind it — but it still holds a quiet, nostalgic charm for anyone passing through.

Fun Fact:

Stockinbingal's railway line makes it one of the key freight routes between Sydney and Perth, quietly playing a vital role in the national transport system despite its small size.

Must See:

- The Commercial Hotel — still standing proud after serving travellers since 1892

- Historic shopfronts — many now closed, but full of character
- Railway junction — Stockinbingal's claim to fame in Australia's freight network

Key Statistics:

- Population: Approx. 244
- Location: South West Slopes, NSW
- Elevation: About 318 metres
- Known for: Historic railway junction, Cobb & Co heritage, classic small-town feel

CHAPTER 75
GUNDAGAI (NSW)

I like Gundagai. It's one of those towns where the past is right there in front of you — not hidden away in a museum but alive and well on the streets themselves. Wandering down Gundagai's main street felt like stepping back in time: I reckon my walk probably wasn't too different to one taken here in the 1980s... or even the early 1900s.

The town clings to the hillside, with levels and slopes that must have caused headaches for architects over the years. Some buildings are perched up on stilts, others dug into the hillside or raised high above it. But there's a good reason for all this oddness: Gundagai had to move.

Originally founded in 1838, the first township was built down on the river flats. A prime spot — or so they thought — until disaster struck on 25 June 1852, when the Murrumbidgee River flooded catastrophically, sweeping the entire town away and killing between 78 and 89 of the 250 residents. It remains one of Australia's deadliest natural disasters. After that, they wisely decided to rebuild halfway up the hill, safely above flood level.

As I continued up the street past charming old shops and verandah-lined buildings, I couldn't help but admire how well-preserved it all felt. No wonder there's a posh caravan park on the edge of town — Gundagai knows how to charm visitors.

At the end of the main street came the real reward: several jaw-dropping attractions. First, there's the Prince Alfred Bridge — a colossal wooden structure and, in true Aussie style, proudly declared the longest timber viaduct in the southern hemisphere. Australians seem particularly fond of these 'southern hemisphere' superlatives — a habit I've noticed you don't hear much in the northern hemisphere, where people simply say 'the biggest' and leave it at that. Built between 1866 and 1869, it was named after Prince Alfred, who'd survived an assassination attempt in Sydney in 1868.

Alongside it runs the old railway bridge, both bridges now in various states of picturesque decay. Part of the road bridge is being preserved, while other sections are deliberately left as a "managed ruin" unless more funding comes through. A little further up the hill, tucked into a cutting, I stumbled upon Gundagai railway station. It's beautifully restored and the setting is pure country idyll — rolling hills, quiet skies, and the peaceful knowledge that no noisy train is going to disturb the view.

After this bit of exploration, I headed back to my accommodation — the aptly named Poet's Recall Motel. Why "Poet's Recall"? Turns out the original Gundagai township had all its streets named after poets. That tradition was lost when the town relocated uphill, but the motel owner has thoughtfully revived the custom by naming all the rooms after famous poets. Lovely touch.

But of course, no mention of Gundagai would be complete without its most famous attraction: the Dog on the Tuckerbox. Now, if you're unfamiliar with this piece of Aussie folklore, you're in for a treat (or perhaps a bit of head-scratching).

The tale goes something like this: a cattle drover named Bullocky Bill was having a rough day. He got bogged down at Nine Mile Creek, then broke the yoke on his bullock team. Just as things couldn't get worse, his faithful dog... well... let's say it "soiled" his tuckerbox (lunchbox).

The story was immortalised in a poem by Bowyang Yorke, later cleaned up in a more family-friendly version by Jack Moses in the 1920s. This quirky little tale captured the imagination of the nation, and in 1932, then Prime Minister Joe Lyons unveiled a statue to commemorate it — located 7km outside Gundagai. It's an iconic bit of Australian kitsch, and a proud symbol of the stoic humour that runs deep in the bush.

Fun Fact:

Gundagai's Dog on the Tuckerbox statue was unveiled by a Prime Minister, no less — Joe Lyons in 1932 — and remains one of Australia's most beloved roadside icons.

Must See:

- Prince Alfred Bridge — historic timber viaduct and landmark

- Gundagai railway station — beautifully restored and atmospheric
- Gundagai's main street — heritage architecture and old-world charm
- Dog on the Tuckerbox — quirky Aussie icon and obligatory photo stop

Key Statistics:

- Population: Approx. 2,000
- Location: South-west slopes of NSW, on the Murrumbidgee River
- Elevation: Roughly 230 metres
- Known for: Heritage streetscape, timber bridges, and of course... that famous dog

CHAPTER 76
ADELONG (NSW)

Adelong's just a short hop from Gundagai, and this little town punches well above its weight when it comes to history. Back in the gold rush days of 1857 to 1876, over 30,000 hopeful souls packed in here, chasing glitter and dreams. Hard to believe now, given that today's Adelong is home to around 900 people and has all the serenity you'd expect from a small country town.

These days it's a tidy, friendly spot, with a few shops and pubs clustered around the heart of town. When I rolled in at 8:30 in the morning, unsurprisingly, not much was happening. The shops were shut, the pubs were shut — even the sleepy dogs looked like they'd taken the morning off. So instead of lingering for retail therapy, I set off on the grandly named "Adelong Cultural Walk," which begins with great promise from Apex Park.

At first, it felt a bit like stepping into *The Wizard of Oz* — concrete paths so clean they could almost have been yellow bricks, leading me forward. The track soon turned rustic though, winding behind the shops and following the riverbank. The river itself might have been reduced to a modest trickle on this particular morning, but there was still a peaceful charm to the scene — the kind of quiet that only a country town can offer.

Still, Adelong didn't let me down. In the park stands a hulking reminder of the town's golden past: a five-tonne gold crushing battery. This bit of serious old mining kit once thundered away, smashing ore to extract every last glimmer of gold. It's now retired and standing proudly on display — a fitting monument to the town's boom-and-bust story.

Fun Fact:

The name "Adelong" is believed to come from an Aboriginal word meaning "along the way" or "river with a billabong."

Must See:

- Adelong Falls Gold Mill Ruins — one of the best-preserved examples of a 19th-century gold processing site.
- Apex Park — where the gold-crushing battery now stands as a memorial to the past.
- Adelong Creek Walk — picturesque in spots, especially near the falls.

Key statistics:

- Population: Around 900
- Known for: Historic gold rush heritage, Adelong Falls Gold Mill ruins
- Location: Snowy Valleys region, New South Wales

CHAPTER 77
JERILDERIE (NSW)

For some time, I'd been keen to visit Ned Kelly's last stand at Glenrowan — and I did, earlier in this trip. But I have to say, if you want a more low-key and less "theme park" experience of Kelly history, Jerilderie is the place to go.

Born in 1854 to Irish immigrant parents, Kelly grew up battling poverty and clashing with authorities in rural Victoria. Kelly's life of crime, fuelled by resentment over perceived injustices against Irish settlers, culminated in a string of robberies, police killings, and his legendary last stand at Glenrowan, clad in homemade iron armour. Whether you see him as villain or victim, there's no doubt Ned Kelly's story is woven deep into Australia's history and identity.

Jerilderie is where Ned Kelly and his gang rode into town on 10 February 1879. They wasted no time making an entrance: capturing the town's two policemen, locking them in their own cell (cheeky), and then dressing up in their uniforms. Clever disguise complete, they roamed the town telling locals they were reinforcements from Sydney, sent to protect them from — you guessed it — the Kelly Gang.

Of course, with the townsfolk suitably duped, the gang wandered into the local bank and relieved it of over two thousand pounds. After that, they chopped down the telegraph poles to cut communications (the 19th-century equivalent of pulling out the Wi-Fi router).

But what really cemented Jerilderie's place in Kelly folklore happened later that evening, when the gang held 30 locals hostage overnight at the Royal Mail Hotel. During this time, Ned sat down and penned what's now known as the Jerilderie Letter — a long, impassioned plea protesting his innocence (despite just having robbed the bank) and setting out his grievances about the treatment of Irish settlers and his family at the hands of the police.

Today's Jerilderie is a far more peaceful affair. It's a classic, sleepy Riverina town that happily welcomes a few tourists keen on Kelly history — and it also has a surprising claim to fame: tomatoes. The area around Jerilderie produces about a quarter of all tomatoes grown in Australia! Not something Ned would have been thinking about as he sharpened his axe on those telegraph poles.

And here's a fun twist: if Gulgong is the $10 town, Jerilderie could easily claim the title of the $100 town, as it was the childhood home of Sir John Monash — the revered military commander whose image graces Australia's $100 note. Not bad for a small town that once got held up by Australia's most famous bushranger.

Fun Fact:

The Jerilderie Letter runs to about 8,000 words — Ned Kelly

certainly wasn't shy when it came to telling his side of the story!

Must See:

- Jerilderie Post and Telegraph Office — still standing and steeped in Kelly history
- Royal Mail Hotel — where the gang held 30 people hostage and where Kelly wrote the Jerilderie Letter
- Jerilderie Letter exhibition — for anyone keen to read Ned's fiery words
- Stroll the quiet streets and spot signs marking key Kelly sites

Key Statistics:

- Population: Approx. 1,000
- Location: Southern Riverina, NSW
- Elevation: Around 100 metres
- Known for: Ned Kelly's 1879 raid, tomatoes, and as the childhood home of Sir John Monash

CHAPTER 78
BILLABONG (VIC)

Ah, Billabong. Such an iconic Aussie word — it crops up everywhere! In fact, there are 59 place names with "Billabong" in New South Wales alone, plus 13 in Queensland, 7 in Victoria and a whopping 86 in the Northern Territory.

Even a Google Maps search gives you a bit of a dilemma: there's a spot simply called "Billabong" deep in the Alpine National Park, well off the Wonnangatta Track — but unless you've got a serious 4WD and a love of bush camping, that one's out of reach for most, including (I'm sure) our travelling "I've been everywhere" man himself.

So I opted for a Billabong that's a tad more accessible: Little Billabong in New South Wales. When I raised this dilemma with Geoff Mack, the bloke who wrote the song, he agreed this was a sensible compromise — even he couldn't quite remember which "Billabong" he had in mind!

Little Billabong is tiny. The heart of this "town" consists of Little Billabong Creek, Little Billabong Village Hall and the

Little Billabong Telephone Exchange. That's about it. I can only assume the other 466 residents are scattered around the surrounding farms and stations — probably keeping a low profile to avoid being counted.

Apparently, Little Billabong even had a post office once, opening its doors on 1 October 1874 and closing them again in 1953 — though I suspect you wouldn't have been queuing long to send a letter there.

These days, there's not much to detain a traveller except for the quiet beauty of the countryside and the satisfaction of ticking "Billabong" off the list. Sometimes, that's enough.

Fun Fact:

No one seems entirely sure which Billabong Geoff Mack had in mind when he wrote *I've Been Everywhere*, but he gave Little Billabong his blessing as a suitable stand-in!

Must See:

- The Little Billabong Village Hall
- The charming Little Billabong Telephone Exchange
- Little Billabong Creek — perfect for... well... standing next to and admiring quietly

Key statistics:

- Population: approx. 466 (but you'd be hard-pressed to find them all at once)
- Location: South West Slopes, NSW — just off the Hume Highway

- Known for: having a lovely name and a very small footprint

CHAPTER 79
YARRA YARRA

Some places I visited on this journey have a thriving pub, a quirky museum or at least a roadhouse sausage roll to write home about. Yarra Yarra, on the other hand... well, let's just say it really tested my imagination.

After much research (and a bit of head-scratching), I tracked Yarra Yarra down as a parish within Goulburn County, NSW — cheers to the Geographical Names Board of NSW. The first time I went looking, all I found was a lonely signpost with just a single *"Yarra"* on it, standing somewhat apologetically by the roadside south of Goulburn.

But the mystery didn't end there. A bit more digging revealed another Yarra Yarra — listed in the NSW Geographical Names Register — sits at latitude -35° 42′ 54.00″ and longitude +147° 27′ 4.00″. For those without a GPS handy: it's a paddock. That's it. A field along Yarra Yarra Road. No pub. No general store. Not even a cow tipped its hat as I passed.

To add to the fun, when I got to meet Geoff Mack himself he remarked that when he wrote the lyrics, he was thinking of the Yarra River — not this windswept paddock. — and something I crossed more than once during the adventure.

Fun Fact:

Despite being immortalised in the song, Yarra Yarra isn't much of a town at all — and Geoff Mack later admitted he was thinking of the Yarra River in Melbourne, not this quiet corner of NSW.

CHAPTER 80
SEYMOUR (VIC)

I rolled into Seymour late in the afternoon, just as the shopkeepers were locking up and pulling down the roller doors — fair enough really, given it felt like the day was winding down altogether. The town centre struck me as a bit quirky, almost lopsided, with all the shops clustered on one side of the main street and the railway station and line on the other. Not a complaint, mind you — just adds to the charm.

A short walk from the centre took me to the town's old wooden lockup, now resting in a park. I can only imagine how stifling it would've been inside that tiny structure on a hot summer's day — not exactly five-star accommodation. It was apparently still in use into the 1960s, so there are probably a few locals around who remember it in action. The lockup has been moved a few times over the years but now sits comfortably next to Seymour's Time Capsule, due to be opened in 2043 to mark the town's 200th anniversary.

Keen for a bit of sightseeing, I asked my motel landlady what else there was to see. She suggested a few local wineries — tempting — and also mentioned the tank museum at nearby

Puckapunyal. Now that sounded interesting. I figured I'd zip over there for a look, knowing full well the museum would be closed at that hour, but hoping to maybe catch a glimpse of a tank or two parked outside.

Little did I realise, Puckapunyal isn't just a place with an army base — it is the army base. The road from Seymour led straight to the guardhouse, and that was it. No town to speak of; just fences, barracks and soldiers.

The poor guard on duty must've thought I was completely daft when I pulled up and asked if the "camp" was open to the public. Thankfully, he quickly clocked that I was harmless (just a curious Pom on a mission) and politely handed me a brochure, explaining that the Australian Army Tank Museum was worth a visit — during proper opening hours, of course.

A bit of history for you: the army base was originally in Seymour during World War I but shifted to Puckapunyal for World War II, and it's remained there ever since. Sensibly, I decided against taking any photos of the military installation — best not to push my luck.

Fun Fact:

Puckapunyal is derived from an Aboriginal word believed to mean "death" or "valley of the spirits" — which feels fitting for a military base if you ask me.

Must See:

- The old wooden lockup in the Seymour park
- Seymour's Time Capsule (due to be opened 2043)

- The Australian Army Tank Museum at Puckapunyal (during opening hours!)

Key statistics:

- Seymour population: approx. 7,000
- Puckapunyal population: army personnel and families
- Location: 100 km north of Melbourne

CHAPTER 81
WANGARATTA (VIC)

I pulled into Wangaratta right on lunchtime, keen to see what this country town had to offer. First stop: the tourist information office — always a good bet for a local tip. Outside stood a large statue of Ned Kelly himself, looking every bit the famous bushranger with bucket helmet and all. Inside, a very cheerful lady popped up from behind the counter, ready to help.

Her suggestions? Gardens and vineyards — but I'm no gardener, and visiting vineyards while driving would only end badly. So she smiled and suggested something a little different: the cemetery. Yep — Wangaratta's "must-see" recommendation was to go grave-hunting!

As I wandered through the town centre toward the cemetery, I couldn't help but notice how bustling Wangaratta was. The place was alive, full of shoppers and without a single boarded-up shopfront — quite a contrast to many country towns I've visited. It honestly felt like Christmas shopping season, except it was March.

On my way out, a sign caught my eye: "Wangaratta, home of the annual Wangaratta Festival of Jazz". Who knew? While Tamworth might lay claim to country music fame, it seems Wangaratta is Australia's jazz capital, and has been since 1990, drawing thousands of festival-goers each year. Not a trumpet or saxophone in sight during my visit though!

Now, onto that cemetery visit. The Wangaratta cemetery is a sprawling place on the southern edge of town. I was there on a mission: to find the grave of Mad Dog Morgan, one of Australia's most notorious bushrangers. Armed with a rough map but no clear sense of direction, I strolled the rows, quietly reading names and pausing at older graves, absorbing the atmosphere and reflecting on the stories buried here.

Eventually, in a peaceful corner near a row of old Chinese graves, I found it: a large stone marker with a brass plaque telling Mad Dog's grim tale. Morgan was infamous for robbing coaches and pastoral stations before finally meeting his end north of Wangaratta in 1865, shot from behind after holding up a homestead. He died at 1:45pm on 9 April 1865 and was buried five days later — but not before his head was removed and sent to the University of Melbourne for anatomical study.

Daniel Morgan's headless body was placed in a pine coffin and buried in the Wangaratta cemetery. A further report states the skin and beard from Morgan's face was made into a tobacco pouch. Morgan was denied a Christian burial; his remains were interred in the Chinese section of the cemetery. A description of his grave published in 1878 noted that a rose-bush and geranium were growing at the head of the grave, planted by Morgan's mother who, up until 1876, had travelled from New South Wales each year to visit the grave.

After my time among the headstones — reflecting on Wangaratta's rich and sometimes brutal past — I jumped back in the car and carried on just 12km down the road to Glenrowan, scene of Ned Kelly's famous final showdown and home to the BIG Ned Kelly.

Fun Fact:

Wangaratta hosts Australia's premier jazz festival — the *Wangaratta Festival of Jazz* — every year since 1990, attracting thousands of music lovers.

Must See:

- Wangaratta's bustling town centre
- Mad Dog Morgan's grave at the Wangaratta Cemetery
- The statue of Ned Kelly and a detour to Glenrowan for the BIG Ned Kelly!

Key Statistics:

- Population: approx. 29,000
- Location: 250km north-east of Melbourne
- Known for: Jazz, Ned Kelly connections, and a lively country town atmosphere.

CHAPTER 82
RIVER MURRAY (NSW)

River Murray or Murray River, or Mighty Murray — take your pick!

Ah, the Mighty Murray. It's one of only two rivers that get a shout-out in *I've Been Everywhere*, and with good reason: at 2,375 kilometres long, it snakes its way from the Australian Alps all the way down to Lake Alexandrina. Safe to say, if you travel long enough in this country, you'll bump into it somewhere.

For me, that somewhere was Albury — a cracking inland town perched on the banks of the Murray and a top spot to soak in a bit of river history. Turns out, this is exactly where Hamilton Hume and William Hovell first crossed the river back in 1824. In true pioneering fashion, they scratched their names (literally) on a tree to mark the occasion — the "Hovell Tree" is still standing today, right there by the river. Not a bad legacy for a bit of bush graffiti.

Now here's where it gets cheeky. When Hume crossed it, he decided to name it after dear old dad — hence, Hume River.

But a few years later, Captain Charles Sturt wandered along, completely unaware that this was the same river Hume and Hovell had encountered upstream, and renamed it the Murray River, after Sir George Murray back in Britain. A classic case of 'right hand not knowing what the left's up to', but the name stuck — and so the Mighty Murray it remains.

Fun Fact

The Murray forms part of Australia's longest continuous river system when combined with its main tributary, the Darling River — 3,672 kilometres.

Must See

- The Hovell Tree: Right on the banks in Albury — a genuine slice of exploration history.
- Murray River precinct: A beautiful spot to stroll, with plenty of shady picnic spots and a few good pubs nearby.
- Albury Botanic Gardens: Not far from the river, these gardens are worth a wander too.

Key Statistics

- Length: 2,375 km
- Source: Australian Alps
- Mouth: Lake Alexandrina, South Australia
- Location visited: Albury, New South Wales

CHAPTER 83
KILMORE (VIC)

I left Seymour early in the morning for Kilmore. It wasn't even light — quite a novelty for me, as I tend to avoid the roads before sunrise or after sunset to steer clear of Australia's famously nocturnal wildlife. No wildlife spotted today though, but I did catch a sunrise — not exactly a postcard-perfect one thanks to some stubborn overcast skies, but still a quietly impressive way to start the day.

It wasn't long after the sun peeked over the horizon that I arrived in Kilmore, where the first thing to catch my eye was the town's leaning sign. "Kilmore" is proudly displayed but on a noticeable lean — a dramatic tilt to the right, in fact. I couldn't help but wonder: is there an undisclosed twinning arrangement between Kilmore and Pisa, Italy?

Kilmore proudly claims the title of Victoria's oldest inland town, so I was curious to see what traces of heritage were still around. Sure enough, dotted along the streets are fine old buildings that bear witness to the town's long history. The first Europeans here were explorers Hamilton Hume and

William Hovell back in 1824 (the same blokes responsible for carving their names into the Hovell Tree in Albury). Thanks to its location near a natural gap in the Dividing Range, Kilmore prospered early on, with traffic passing through en route to Melbourne.

One of the more striking remnants of Kilmore's past is its old Gaol (yes, spelt the Aussie way). Opened in 1859 as a maximum-security prison, it later had a surprising career change — becoming a butter factory in 1891, then a private residence, and now a tourist attraction. I couldn't help but chuckle at the image of hardened criminals once pacing those bluestone walls... only for them to later churn out butter.

I also wandered past the bluestone Post Office (opened in 1843) and Court House — fine examples of colonial architecture and a reminder of Kilmore's early significance. It's one of those towns that rewards a slow walk and a good look around — history is literally written in its stones.

Fun Fact:

Kilmore's name may come from the Irish *"Cill Mór"*, meaning "great church," reflecting the strong Irish influence in the early settlement.

Must See:

- Kilmore's Old Gaol (turned butter factory!)
- Bluestone Post Office and Courthouse
- Main Street's colonial architecture

Key statistics:

- Population: approx. 8,000
- Location: 60 km north of Melbourne
- Known for: Victoria's oldest inland town, colonial architecture, historic buildings

CHAPTER 84
DANDENONG (VIC)

I left the tranquillity of *Kilmore* (still shaking off its morning slumber) and before long, I was back on the *Hume Highway*, heading south towards *Dandenong* — a large city on the outskirts of Melbourne.

As I got closer, the contrast couldn't have been more stark. The serenity of the outback roads was soon a distant memory, replaced by ever-thickening traffic. I noticed huge roadside timers flashing estimated travel times to various points ahead — as though designed to keep us drivers from losing patience completely. Standing there in my car queue, I couldn't help but feel like an egg in a giant urban boiling pot... and I was definitely starting to miss the endless open roads behind me.

If it was solitude I was after, I wasn't going to find it in *Dandenong*. Often described as Melbourne's equivalent of *Parramatta* in Sydney — a major satellite hub in its own right — Dandenong was buzzing with life. It happened to be *Market Day* too, and a throng of people was swarming around rows of colourful stalls, all busy buying everything from fresh produce to curiosities.

I wandered around for a bit, soaking it all in, before settling on an essential purchase: a couple of bones for the dog (because, priorities!).

Afterwards, I crossed the road and meandered through the main shopping centre and along the high street, pausing to appreciate the curious "concrete sofa" installation that sat proudly on the footpath — Dandenong's answer to urban street art, apparently.

After all the quiet country towns I'd visited, Dandenong felt like a jolt back into modern suburban life — busy, bustling, multicultural, and well and truly alive.

Fun Fact:

Dandenong's market has been running since 1866, making it one of the oldest continuously operating markets in Victoria.

Must See:

- Dandenong Market — one of Melbourne's oldest and most diverse markets
- High street shopping and street art installations (including that concrete sofa)
- Dandenong Plaza for an indoor wander and a bite to eat

Key statistics:

- Population: approx. 30,000 (city proper; part of Greater Dandenong, around 160,000)
- Location: 30 km southeast of Melbourne CBD
- Known for: vibrant multicultural community, historic market, gateway to Gippsland

CHAPTER 85
GEELONG (VIC)

From a distance, I thought I was going to really enjoy *Geelong*. You see, I took the road marked "scenic route" into this seaside town and was treated to a sweeping view across the bay — including the impressive *Cunningham Pier*. And for a brief, optimistic moment I wondered: could this be Australia's answer to *Blackpool*?

The sight of a long pier jutting proudly into the water had me dreaming of "Kiss Me Quick" hats, jars of cockles, candy floss, and a rickety funfair at the end. So, with visions of seaside frivolity dancing in my head, I steered into town, parked up, and made my way toward the grand theatrical entrance of the pier.

With every step I took down its length, my anticipation grew. Surely at the end there'd be the cheery chaos of sideshows and souvenir shops? Alas... no.

While the view from the pier was cracking, and judging by the number of fishermen it must have been a decent spot for a catch, this was not quite the pleasure pier I'd been hoping for. There was no candy floss, no dodgem cars, no amusement arcades filled with chiming machines. Instead, waiting for me at the end was a restaurant and a conference centre — not exactly the riot of fun I'd pictured.

As it turns out, *Cunningham Pier* was built for far more practical reasons. From the 1920s through the 1950s, this was a working pier, bustling not with tourists but with inbound coal shipments. It fell into disuse for a time before getting a makeover in the late 1990s, transforming it into a more leisurely promenade — but without the sticks of rock or ghost trains.

Even without a bucket and spade vibe, there's no denying Geelong's waterfront is a lovely spot for a wander — a working port with history and a dash of modern charm. So while it wasn't Blackpool, it still made for an enjoyable stop.

Fun Fact:

Cunningham Pier was named after Captain Cunningham, a local ship owner and entrepreneur. While it's not a funfair hub, it remains a key part of Geelong's maritime heritage.

Must See:

- Cunningham Pier and its sweeping bay views
- Geelong Waterfront precinct — ideal for a stroll
- The Bollard Trail sculptures along the foreshore

Key statistics:

- Population: approx. 270,000 (Victoria's second largest city)
- Location: 75 km southwest of Melbourne
- Known for: vibrant waterfront, AFL's Geelong Cats, gateway to the Bellarine Peninsula and Great Ocean Road

CHAPTER 86
BALLARAT (VIC)

I'd already crossed paths with Australia's gold rush history when I visited *Gulgong* — a town that cashed in towards the *tail end* of the rush — but *Ballarat* is where it all kicked off. Gold was first discovered here in 1851, just a few miles from the town centre, and before you could say *"strike it rich"*, over 10,000 hopeful miners had descended, picks and pans in hand.

But it wasn't all gold dust and glory. Life on the goldfields was tough, unfair licensing laws angered the miners, and tensions boiled over into the infamous *Eureka Stockade* on 3 December 1854 — Australia's most famous rebellion and a defining chapter in the nation's democratic story.

Ballarat still wears its gold rush history proudly. Many grand buildings from that era remain, like the imposing *Gold Exchange*, but rather than wander the real streets, I decided to take a little detour... into *Sovereign Hill*.

Sovereign Hill is like stepping into a time machine — a beautifully reconstructed 1850s goldfields town, built in the 1960s and opened in 1970. And honestly? It's amazing.

The whole place hums with life: staff in period costume wander dusty streets, there are mine tours, working blacksmiths, sweet shops, old-timey schools, and even *Cobb & Co* coaches rattling along the road. Everything I'd read and imagined about gold rush life was brought vividly to life here.

Next door, the *Gold Museum* kept me equally entertained, with displays of glittering gold in every shape and form — from coins to jewellery to massive nuggets.

Speaking of nuggets, one of Ballarat's real claims to fame is the extraordinary *Welcome Nugget*, discovered by a Cornish miner in 1858. Weighing in at 69 kilograms (that's almost the weight of an adult human!) and worth £10,500 at the time, it remains the *second largest gold nugget ever found.*

Just imagine being the lucky bloke who dug that up — and then imagine trying to carry it home!

Fun Fact:

The *Welcome Nugget* found in Ballarat was so huge, it weighed nearly 70 kg — that's heavier than a full-grown labrador — and was valued at a fortune even back in 1858.

Must See:

- *Sovereign Hill*: a brilliant living history experience
- *Gold Museum*: shining examples of Ballarat's golden past
- Ballarat's historic buildings, including the *Gold Exchange*

Key statistics:

- Population: approx. 110,000
- Location: Central Victoria
- Known for: Australia's richest gold rush history, Eureka Stockade, beautifully preserved heritage buildings

CHAPTER 87
BENDIGO (VIC)

Another early start meant another early arrival — this time into *Bendigo*.

Like Ballarat, Bendigo owes its very existence to gold. You can't help but be impressed by the sheer grandeur of this town; the wide streets are lined with extravagant Victorian buildings that ooze wealth and confidence — a reminder of the golden spoils that built them.

Although mining officially ceased in 1954, Bendigo couldn't quite shake off its gold fever. *Bendigo Mining Ltd* recommenced operations in 2006, briefly pulling more treasure from the earth at Kangaroo Flat — though limited reserves saw them pack it in just eight months later. In that short time, they managed to process nearly 176,000 tonnes of ore and produce 26,735 ounces of gold. Not bad for a second crack.

For visitors, the big drawcard these days is the *Central Deborah Gold Mine*, where you can don a hard hat and descend 61 metres below ground. This mine, which operated from 1939 to 1954, was the last commercial mine to close on the Bendigo goldfields before modern operations restarted. Today it offers a brilliant chance to experience what life was like down a real gold mine — without having to wield a pickaxe yourself.

Bendigo feels like a place where history sits proudly on display but hasn't stood still — heritage buildings, gold rush stories, and modern coffee culture all sharing space in this grand old town.

Fun Fact:

Bendigo's goldfields produced over *700,000 kilograms of gold* during the boom years — making it one of the richest goldfields in the world.

Must See:

- The *Central Deborah Gold Mine* tour — 61 metres underground and packed with history
- Grand Victorian streetscapes — the architecture alone is worth a wander
- Bendigo's excellent cafés and bakeries for a well-earned break

Key statistics:

- Population: approx. 100,000
- Location: Central Victoria, about 150 km northwest of Melbourne
- Known for: gold rush heritage, stunning Victorian architecture, rich cultural history

CHAPTER 88
DENILIQUIN (NSW)

As you drive into Deniliquin, you can't help but notice one thing — it's flat. Very flat. Flatter than Captains Flat and flatter than just about anything else I've driven through. That's no accident: Deniliquin sits on the famous Hay Plains, an area that proudly claims the smallest deviation of elevation on Earth. If you ever wanted to experience what it's like to drive across a billiard table, this is the place.

So what do you do with all this flatness? Well, I decided the best approach was to head straight to the Peppin Heritage Centre, which handily doubles as the Visitor Information Centre. The building itself is a lovely bit of history — Deniliquin's first public school — and still has one of its original classrooms intact, complete with those old wooden desks that brought back a few uncomfortable memories of childhood days spent trying to stay awake during lessons.

Inside, there's a museum devoted to the district's history, tracing Deniliquin's evolution from a wool-growing stronghold to its modern agricultural identity, including the impressive rise of rice farming in the area. One exhibit introduces the Deniliquin Rice Mill, apparently the largest in the Southern Hemisphere. Not bad for a place that looks like it could disappear into the horizon in every direction.

The museum also celebrates the Peppin family, whose legacy I discovered in more detail during my visit to nearby Wanganella — but suffice to say they left quite a mark on this part of the country.

Fun Fact:

Deniliquin holds the Guinness World Record for the largest parade of legally registered utes, thanks to the annual Deni Ute Muster — a proper outback festival if ever there was one.

Must See:

- Peppin Heritage Centre
- Deniliquin Rice Mill (or at least learn about it at the museum)
- Wander along the Edward River for a peaceful stroll
- Check out Ute on the Pole, a quirky local icon celebrating Deniliquin's famous Ute Muster

Key Statistics:

- Population: Approx. 7,500
- Location: Southern Riverina, New South Wales
- Elevation: Roughly 90 metres — but you wouldn't know it
- Known for: Wool, rice, and utes!

CHAPTER 89
WANGANELLA (NSW)

A bit of a detour up the Cobb Highway landed me in Wanganella — a tiny village that, to be fair, doesn't offer much for the casual visitor. But I'd been tipped off by the helpful lady at the Deniliquin Tourist Information Centre about Wanganella's surprising claim to fame: this unassuming spot is the birthplace of the legendary *Peppin Merino*.

Back in 1861, George Hall Peppin and his two sons — English sheep breeders with plenty of experience — set up a Merino stud at Wanganella Station, just north of Deniliquin. The Peppins set to work developing a hardy new line of sheep capable of thriving in the tough, dry inland conditions. The result? The Peppin Merino, a sheep that would go on to dominate Australian wool production.

In fact, it's said that today around 70% of all Merinos in Australia can trace their lineage directly back to those first Wanganella sheep — an extraordinary legacy for such a small place.

Sheep farming being what it is — proud, passionate and resilient — local graziers have marked this achievement with a bronze statue of a Peppin Merino right here in Wanganella. It's a fine piece of work and probably the village's one standout attraction — a perfect photo stop if you're passing through.

Other than the statue and a healthy sense of rural history, there's not much else to detain you. But as with many places on this journey, it's the stories behind these seemingly ordinary dots on the map that make them worth visiting.

Fun Fact:

The Peppin Merino didn't just adapt to Australia's dry interior — it transformed the country's wool industry, helping Australia become the world's largest wool producer.

Must See:

- The bronze Peppin Merino statue — paying tribute to an Aussie icon
- Wanganella Station's historic role in Australian wool history (viewed from the roadside)

Key statistics:

- Population: approx. 30 (yes, really!)
- Location: on the Cobb Highway, north of Deniliquin
- Known for: birthplace of the Peppin Merino sheep

CHAPTER 90
GRONG GRONG (NSW)

Grong Grong is one of those tiny rural villages that dot the highway and quietly invite curiosity. Well, I stopped. And while it's true that Grong Grong probably isn't on most travellers' bucket lists, it has a quiet charm — if you take the time to look.

The town is small. Really small. The highlights are classic country Australia: a pub (naturally), a church, a few grain silos standing tall over the flat plains, and a railway line that's been still for years. The disused railway and empty grain bins hint at Grong Grong's past — a time when small railway towns like this were vital links in the agricultural supply chain.

The name itself is a cracker. Grong Grong comes from an Aboriginal term meaning "bad camping ground" or even "very bad camping ground" — which makes you smile and wonder what early travellers encountered here. But these days, it's the quirky name that puts Grong Grong on the map (and probably earns more photos than any of its buildings).

Wandering around, it was hard not to appreciate the slower rhythm of life here. A few locals waved as they went about their day, with that typical small-town friendliness — stay a while and you'd likely hear a few good yarns at the pub.

Grong Grong might not offer grand tourist attractions, but it's places like this that remind you of Australia's rural backbone: small communities, grain silos on the skyline, and a proud history of resilience in a tough landscape.

Fun Fact:

Rugby league legend **Peter Sterling** grew up here before making it big with the Parramatta Eels and on TV — proof that even the smallest places can produce big stars.

Must See:

- Grong Grong Hotel — classic country pub, even if it's just for a photo
- Grain silos — striking against the endless Riverina sky
- The old railway line — an echo of the town's former role as a transport hub

Key Statistics:

- Population: Around 250
- Location: Riverina region, NSW, on the Newell Highway
- Elevation: Approx. 150 metres
- Known for: Its memorable name and classic "blink-and-you'll-miss-it" country town vibe

CHAPTER 91
DARWIN (NT)

Travelling around Australia has taught me plenty about Aussie resilience — but spending a few days in Darwin takes that lesson to a whole new level. Sure, any Australian can cope with a bit of heat and humidity, but Darwin's locals have endured a lot more than sweaty weather: devastating cyclones and World War II bombings literally flattened this city not once, but several times. If survival were a national sport, the people of Darwin would be champions.

The last time Darwin was levelled was Christmas Eve 1974, when *Cyclone Tracy* tore through the city with 200 mph winds, leaving almost nothing standing. That explains why Darwin today looks so fresh and modern — most of what you see has been rebuilt since 1974. A handful of older buildings do remain, like the skeletal ruins of the old Town Hall, which were scattered far and wide by Tracy's fury. Fittingly, bits of its doors and windows now reside safely at the *Museum and Art Gallery of the Northern Territory* (MAGNT), alongside excellent displays about Cyclone Tracy itself. The museum is also home to a brilliant collection of Aboriginal art and local wildlife exhibits — I could have easily spent half a day wandering through its cool halls.

Long before Cyclone Tracy, Darwin was on the receiving end of another disaster: Japanese air raids on 19 February 1942 — the largest foreign attacks ever mounted against Australia. The bombing left the town in ruins again, with further attacks continuing throughout the war years. While many European women and children were evacuated, the Aboriginal community remained, adding to the remarkable resilience of this town.

That wartime history is preserved in some unique ways. One of my favourites was visiting the *WWII Oil Storage Tunnels*— built beneath Darwin to store fuel safely out of bombing range. Seven tunnels were planned, but only five were completed thanks to material shortages and difficulties waterproofing the rock. Today, you can peer into one tunnel and walk the length of another, with historic photographs lining the walls as you go. It's a cool and atmospheric way to get a feel for Darwin's wartime past (and a nice break from the heat, too!).

Exploring the tunnels left me wanting more history, so I took a short drive out to *East Point Reserve*. This area was once a heavily fortified military site and still features the remains of bunkers, gun emplacements and fortifications. I particularly enjoyed clambering around a massive coastal gun bunker designed to defend Darwin Harbour from a Japanese sea assault — a battle that, thankfully, never came. Ironically, the giant gun itself was sold as scrap metal to the Japanese after the war... which feels like a classic twist in the Australian story.

Of course, cyclones aren't Darwin's only natural hazard. The waterways around the city are teeming with crocodiles — proper saltwater crocs that don't muck around. I took a boat trip up the *Adelaide River* where these prehistoric beasts put on quite a show, launching themselves out of the water to snap at hunks of pork dangled enticingly from a stick. Let's just say I was very careful to keep all my limbs safely inside the boat at all times!

Another highlight was the *Aviation Heritage Centre*, a fascinating collection of aircraft and aviation memorabilia salvaged after Cyclone Tracy. Taking pride of place is a massive Boeing B-52 bomber — a rare sight and worth the visit on its own.

When I needed a break from history and crocs, Darwin didn't disappoint. The *George Brown Darwin Botanic Gardens* offered a peaceful retreat close to town, while nearby *Litchfield National Park* proved an absolute gem — waterfalls, rock pools and giant termite mounds aplenty. It was a great way to unwind before heading home. Kakadu National Park is also within reach but deserves far more than a quick dash, so I left that for another adventure.

In the end, four days in Darwin felt just right — enough time to soak up its fascinating history, appreciate its tropical vibe and marvel at the resilience of a city that's been flattened, bombed and battered, yet always manages to rise again.

Fun Fact:

Darwin has been struck by major cyclones at least once every few decades — almost a rite of passage for each generation of residents.

Must See:

- Museum and Art Gallery of the Northern Territory (MAGNT)
- WWII Oil Storage Tunnels
- East Point Reserve and military relics
- Darwin Harbour and waterfront precinct
- Adelaide River jumping crocodile cruise
- Aviation Heritage Centre (don't miss the B-52 bomber!)
- Litchfield National Park: waterfalls, rock pools, and termite mounds

Key statistics:

- Population: approx. 150,000
- Location: Northern Territory, Australia's tropical Top End
- Known for: tropical climate, wartime history, Cyclone Tracy, crocodiles, and incredible national parks

CHAPTER 92
TIBOOBURRA (NSW)

Broken Hill

After a break of a few months — thanks to more rain than the Murray's seen in a while and a fair few roads underwater — I finally hit the road again. The skies cleared, the bitumen dried, and I was off. I did toy with the idea of flying into some places, but that's on hold for now. Birdsville's still tempting me — although at this point it might be easier to swim there.

Now, technically, Broken Hill isn't one of the 94 places named in *I've Been Everywhere*, but it was my ideal base camp for the next leg of my journey — especially for my day trip up to Tibooburra. And honestly, Broken Hill's too much of an outback icon to skip over, so it deserves a spot here.

It's tucked away some 1,147 kilometres west of Sydney on the Barrier Highway, and it sits so close to the South Australian border that it cheekily adopts SA time — half an hour behind Sydney. One of those delightful quirks you find in

Australia where a New South Wales town just shrugs and says, "yeah nah, we'll run on Adelaide time, thanks."

I rolled into town mid-morning, giving me enough time to stretch my legs around the place and then duck out to Silverton, that legendary outback hamlet about 20 kilometres north. Silverton has its own vibe — part film set, part ghost town, part pub stop.

Travelling with Amelie, my loyal Cavalier, meant I was on the lookout for dog-friendly digs. I was fortunate to get pointed towards the Caledonian, where Hugh and Barbara run not only a B&B but also a few cottages around town. Their hospitality was top-notch, and Amelie gave it the paw of approval too — always a good sign.

Mullock

You can't miss Broken Hill's most striking feature: those massive man-made mullock heaps that dominate the skyline. Locals proudly compare them to Uluru — especially when they glow red and orange in the evening sun. Not bad for a giant pile of mining waste!

And for all its mining history, Broken Hill doesn't feel overly industrial. The streets are tidy, and the place has a certain well-kept charm. But if you pay attention, the street names give it away: Chloride, Cobalt, Sulphide and Bromide Streets... a nod to the minerals that put this place on the map.

The fortunes of mining have waxed and waned here over the years. After all, this is the birthplace of BHP — the Broken Hill Proprietary Company — now a global mining giant. But Broken Hill hasn't just relied on the mines to define itself. These days, it leans into its artistic side, too.

The town was home to the legendary Pro Hart, often called the 'father of outback painting'. His colourful, sometimes cheeky artworks put the Aussie bush on canvas in a way nobody had before. The local sculpture scene is impressive too — especially the Living Desert Sculptures, best viewed at sunset when the light puts on a show almost as good as the artwork itself.

Fun Fact

Broken Hill is so culturally and historically significant that it became Australia's first heritage-listed city — a nod to its unique blend of mining grit, outback character and artistic flair.

Must See

- Line of Lode Miners Memorial: Sitting atop the mullock heap, it's both a sobering monument and a stunning lookout over the town.
- Pro Hart Gallery: A must for art lovers (and even those who aren't) — Pro's work captures the outback spirit like no one else.
- Living Desert Sculptures: A striking outdoor gallery set among the rocky desert hills, with sunset views that are worth the drive.

Key Statistics

- Location: 1,147 km west of Sydney on the Barrier Highway

- Population: Approx. 17,000
- Time zone: Australian Central Standard Time (30 minutes behind Sydney)
- Elevation: 315 metres above sea level
- Claim to fame: Birthplace of BHP and home to Pro Hart, with more pubs than you could visit in a weekend.

Silverton

I couldn't resist the chance to detour from Broken Hill and check out Silverton — this quirky little outback icon. Surreal, dusty, artistic, crazy and friendly... all those adjectives fit, but they still don't quite capture what it's like wandering its wide, sandy streets. It's one of those places that's both appealing and a little baffling to visitors.

You find yourself wondering: is this a serious town or some kind of themed tourist attraction? These days, I reckon it's definitely the latter. Silverton's original claim to fame was silver mining, but like so many outback towns, the boom didn't last. When the massive silver-lead-zinc deposits were discovered over at Broken Hill, Silverton's fate was sealed — it was quickly eclipsed and largely abandoned.

But Silverton didn't fade away entirely. Instead, it morphed into something else — an artistic outpost and a favourite for film crews needing a ready-made outback backdrop. It's got that quintessential dusty-desert look and it's close enough to civilisation (well, Broken Hill) to be convenient.

The place has starred in more films and TV shows than some actors. *The Adventures of Priscilla, Queen of the Desert, The*

Flying Doctors, *Dirty Deeds*... they've all passed through here. And it shows — everywhere you turn there's a wink to its time in the spotlight.

It's the sort of town where a friendly local at the pub will happily tell you that *Mad Max 2* was filmed just down the road, right before pouring you a cold one and offering to show you where the iconic scenes were shot.

Silverton's got an artistic heart too — from dusty old galleries to rusted sculptures scattered about. It feels a bit like an outback movie set that people decided to keep living in... and why not? There's a certain charm to it all.

Fun Fact

Silverton's population once peaked at around 3,000 during the mining boom — today, fewer than 50 people call it home, but it still attracts thousands of visitors every year.

Must See

• Silverton Hotel: A classic outback pub with movie memorabilia plastered across the walls and a cold beer waiting for you.

• Mad Max Museum: Dedicated entirely to *Mad Max 2*, this quirky little collection is run by die-hard fans.

• Local art galleries: Scattered through town, these showcase bold, desert-inspired works — well worth a wander.

• Penrose Park: A shady green spot nearby, perfect for a break if you're travelling with a dog or just want a breather from the red dust.

. . .

Key Statistics

- Location: 25 km north-west of Broken Hill
- Population: Less than 50 permanent residents
- Elevation: 300 metres above sea level
- Claim to fame: Filming location for *Mad Max 2*, *Priscilla, Queen of the Desert*, and more.

———

Tibooburra

I hit the road to Tibooburra early, heading out after sunrise from Broken Hill — not because I'm a morning person, but in the hope I'd avoid any kamikaze kangaroos bounding across the road. The journey itself was classic outback: a mix of sealed and unsealed stretches, all pretty good going, and very little traffic apart from the odd roadwork crew.

Tibooburra, bless it, is marketed for its "arid landscape" and "remarkable granite rock outcrops". Hardly the sort of thing that'll have the tourists flooding in — unless you've got a real passion for rocks and dust. Funnily enough, the town's name actually comes from an Aboriginal word meaning *heap of boulders*, which feels... quite accurate.

But there's more to this little place than first impressions. Tibooburra is known as the capital of *Corner Country* — that remote patch of outback where New South Wales, Queensland and South Australia all meet at Cameron Corner. In fact, with a bit of creative positioning, you can stand at Cameron Corner and hit a golf ball across all three states in one swing. That's a pretty unique claim to fame.

The village itself is what you'd expect from a remote outback town: dusty, quiet, but tidy. I stopped in at the garage/general store, which — as is typical of the bush — stocked everything from engine oil to tinned peaches and a pretty impressive selection in between. After that, I took a wander through town where the highlights included the Tibooburra Outback School of the Air. This place delivers education both on-site and remotely via radio and internet to kids scattered across vast cattle stations — an incredible example of bush ingenuity. The other local institution is, of course, the Tibooburra Hotel: a classic outback pub and heart of the community.

Having seen what Tibooburra had to offer, I couldn't resist detouring back down the Silver City Highway to Milparinka, a near-ghost town these days but once a bustling base for gold miners heading out to Mount Browne. The historic buildings are mostly ruins now but dotted with information plaques telling stories of gold rush days and tough lives.

I pressed on another 18km along a rough dirt track to the Mount Browne goldfields themselves. I have to say, the landscape was rugged and atmospheric, but sadly no nuggets leapt into my hand. I spotted one lone bloke up on the hill with a metal detector — maybe he was having better luck than me.

With my pockets still empty, it was time to call it a day and head back down the highway for a good night's sleep in Broken Hill, before setting my sights on the penultimate destination of this whole adventure: Oodnadatta.

Fun Fact:

At Cameron Corner, golfers sometimes have a crack at teeing off across three states with a single shot — a true Aussie pastime!

Must See:

- Cameron Corner: stand in three states at once
- Tibooburra Hotel
- Tibooburra Outback School of the Air
- Milparinka Heritage Precinct
- Mount Browne goldfields (even if you don't strike it rich)

Key statistics:

- Tibooburra population: approx. 150
- Location: far north-west New South Wales
- Main industries: tourism, grazing, and outback services
- Corner Country sits close to the intersection of NSW, QLD, and SA borders

CHAPTER 93
OODNADATTA (SA)

Coober Pedy

Now, Coober Pedy isn't in the *I've Been Everywhere* song, but it certainly earned an honourable mention on my journey. In fact, it served as my 'base camp' before heading deeper into the outback towards Oodnadatta. And let's face it — you can't pass this way without stopping for a look. After all, this is the self-proclaimed *Opal Capital of the World* and home to those famous underground dwellings.

I rolled into town after a decent stint on the road, having driven up from Pilba — 366 kilometres south — where I'd stayed overnight at a campsite. As soon as you approach Coober Pedy, it's impossible to miss the sheer evidence of mining all around: endless mounds of spoil — piles of dirt, rock, and rubble — scattered across the landscape like a giant had been digging for treasure (which, essentially, they have). The main street offers the typical outback essentials: petrol stations, a supermarket, a chemist, a bank, the all-important tourist information office, and plenty of shops eager to sell you freshly mined opals, from humble stones to eye-wateringly expensive jewellery.

Venture just a block off the main drag and the sealed road gives way to dust, and the mounds take on a different form: they're homes. Yes, people really do live underground here — not just a quirky gimmick for tourists but a clever response to the brutal desert climate. When summer temperatures soar beyond 40°C, the locals stay cool by burrowing into the hillsides. Down here, it's a comfortable, steady temperature all year round. No air-con needed — nature's insulation does the trick.

I was lucky enough to book myself into an underground room at the aptly named Desert View Apartments along Catacomb Road. My room was essentially a long tunnel cut straight into the hillside, with a bathroom block and a sturdy door attached at the entrance. Surprisingly spacious and bright, thanks to the whitewashed walls that reflected what little light there was, it didn't feel claustrophobic in the slightest. It was peaceful too — the outside world muffled by metres of solid rock.

At about 24°C outside during my visit, I didn't notice any change in temperature inside the room at all — cool, comfortable and constant. Perfect sleeping conditions, I thought. And it was almost perfectly silent as well, apart from the occasional faint bark of a dog somewhere in town, echoing its way down the ventilation pipe above my room. And though I expected pitch-black darkness, I soon realised the soft glow from the doorway kept the gloom at bay (my fault for leaving the door ajar!).

Still, I slept like a log — no distractions, no worries — the quiet, cool sanctuary of the underground doing exactly what it was designed to do. You have to admire the ingenuity of life in this part of Australia: if you can't beat the heat, dig your way under it.

Fun Fact:

The name *Coober Pedy* comes from the local Aboriginal term *kupa-piti*, meaning *white man's hole*. Apt, really!

Must See:

- Umoona Opal Mine and Museum — learn the history and browse opals
- The underground Serbian Orthodox Church — beautifully carved right into the rock
- Coober Pedy Golf Course — yes, a golf course, but don't expect much grass!
- Josephine's Gallery and Kangaroo Orphanage

Key statistics:

- Location: Approx. 850 km north of Adelaide
- Population: Around 1,700 hardy souls
- Known for: Opals, underground homes, extreme climate

Oodnadata

"Well, I was humpin' my bluey on the dusty Oodnadatta road…" — the very first place mentioned in the song, and the one I was most looking forward to.

The night before heading off, I felt like a kid on Christmas Eve — except I was lying awake in an underground hole in Coober Pedy, listening to the desert silence and picturing 189 km of dirt track ahead.

Oodnadatta is remote — properly remote — so after two punctures elsewhere on this trip, I wasn't taking any chances: new tyres, a good spare, repair kits, a Personal Locator Beacon, and a mate back home tracking my progress.

I set off just after sunrise, giving the kangaroos time to clear off — let's face it, they're not known for using pedestrian crossings out here. Soon I hit the legendary Oodnadatta Track, recently reopened after months of flooding. A few washouts kept things interesting but it was in surprisingly good nick.

The road itself was a surprise — changing colour constantly: red, white, grey, black — depending on what material had been used for repairs. The landscape, too, kept shifting: scrub to grassland, flat plains to distant hills, all starkly beautiful.

After about three hours bumping along, I reached the real Oodnadatta Track junction, turned left — and there it was: Oodnadatta.

Tiny but iconic, this is the kind of place you can walk from one end to the other in five minutes. At its heart is the famous Pink Roadhouse — not just pink, but a proper outback institution. Despite being deep in woop woop, it was buzzing with 4WD travellers fuelling up, stocking supplies and taking a break from the corrugations.

I did the sensible thing: ordered the "Oodnadatta burger with the lot" — stacked with lettuce, beef, cheese, pineapple, bacon and beetroot (because we Aussies love putting beetroot on burgers).

Burger sorted, I wandered over some old disused railway tracks to the Oodnadatta Museum, in the original train station. This was once a bustling railway town — the northern terminus of the Great Northern Railway in 1890, until the line pushed on to Alice Springs in 1929. By 1981, the railway had shifted west altogether, leaving Oodnadatta's rail glory days in the dust.

These days, tourism keeps it alive — that and its legend as a classic outback stop. Just over 200 hardy souls live here, and the place thrives as a spot for travellers to stop for a burger, a refuel and a yarn.

Other than that? Not a whole lot to do — and that's exactly how it should be. After a nosey around town, I picked up my metaphorical bluey and bumped my way back along that dusty track to my underground haven in Coober Pedy.

Fun Fact:

The Oodnadatta Track was once part of the original route of *The Ghan railway*, a vital supply line through some of Australia's most remote country.

Must See:

- The iconic *Pink Roadhouse* — fuel, supplies, burgers and plenty of character
- The *Oodnadatta Museum* at the old railway station
- The rainbow-hued *Oodnadatta Track* itself — an outback road trip essential

Key statistics:

- Population: approx. 200
- Location: Far north South Australia, on the edge of the Simpson Desert
- Known for: Pink Roadhouse, railway history, outback legend status

CHAPTER 94
BIRDSVILLE (QLD)

After 642 days and around 30,000 km crisscrossing Australia, I finally rolled into Birdsville — the 94th and last location in the lyrics of that iconic song. Birdsville sits right at the border of South Australia and Queensland, about 1,590 km west of Brisbane, and a whopping 2,000 km from home at Terrigal... which, of course, meant another 2,000 km just to get back again!

This last leg was always going to be special. I wasn't travelling solo either — joining me were my 86-year-old mother, my 19-year-old niece Emily (both visiting from the UK), my partner Billy, and our four-year-old cavalier, Amelie. As one motel owner put it, we made for a strange mix of travellers — but it's probably what made this trip so fun.

For this journey, I swapped my trusty Tiguan for a Toyota LandCruiser — a wise move, given four passengers, camping gear, remote country, and hazards such as stone chips and the occasional suicidal emu (one did test our reflexes en route). The LandCruiser proved a perfect companion for the wild west.

The road to Birdsville took us through a long list of towns — Hunter Valley, Dubbo, Narromine, Nyngan, Bourke, Cunnamulla, Charleville, Quilpie, and Windorah — before finally reaching Birdsville itself. We stayed in campsites along the way, opting for cabins for Mum's comfort (and our sanity). It's amazing to think that even in the middle of nowhere you can usually find a bed for the night — a testament to how many Aussies these days are embracing outback travel.

As you head inland, the transformation is striking — lush green fields giving way to sandy scrub, flocks of birds giving way to soaring eagles, emus by the roadside, and kangaroos bounding out unexpectedly (always a thrill, and a hazard). For much of the way, the roads were surprisingly good — wide, sealed, and in great nick — until the last 200 km, where they turned into a proper outback challenge: bone-shaking, dusty and rough. We were all a bit relieved when that final stretch was behind us.

We'd timed the trip so we didn't have to rush — but ironically arrived the day *after* the famous Birdsville Races. The town still had a real buzz about it, with the population swollen well beyond its usual 300 souls. Most visitors were still hanging around, and judging by the crowds at the *Birdsville Pub* and the *Birdsville Bakery*, they weren't in a hurry to leave either.

Naturally, we stopped in at both institutions. Mum and Billy tucked into kangaroo pies at the bakery — I swear they walked with extra spring in their step afterwards!

Birdsville itself truly felt like a fitting finale for this journey — the quintessential outback town. The locals were warm, welcoming, and friendly, just as they'd been all across regional Australia. Whether it was walking down the street or popping into a shop or bakery, every encounter was met with a smile or a yarn.

We visited the ruins of the old *Royal Hotel*, which once served as one of three pubs in Birdsville but was later converted into a hospital — materials for its construction famously hauled into town by a caravan of 75 camels. A drive out of town took us to the remarkable *Waddi Trees*, one of only three places in Australia where they grow. These trees are legendary for their timber — so tough it breaks axes and saws.

With no beds available in Birdsville thanks to the race crowds, we hit the road again that afternoon, heading back to Windorah where a room was waiting. Over the following days, we wound our way back home via Quilpie, Charleville, Mitchell, St George, Mungindi, Moree, Narrabri, Gunnedah, Tamworth and the Hunter Valley — enjoying the long road home, knowing that the adventure had come full circle.

Fun Fact:

The Waddi Trees found near Birdsville are so dense and tough that their timber can blunt axes and break saw blades. They're also among the oldest trees in the desert, some estimated to be over 1,000 years old.

Must See:

- Birdsville Pub — an Australian outback icon
- Birdsville Bakery — kangaroo pies and classic bush treats
- The old Royal Hotel ruins
- Waddi Trees — some of the hardest timber in the country

- The vast desert landscape surrounding the town

Key statistics:

- Population: approx. 300
- Location: far west Queensland, on the edge of the Simpson Desert
- Known for: Birdsville Races, legendary pub, remote outback spirit

EPILOGUE

And so, after criss-crossing deserts, coasts, backroads, and bustling towns, my journey came to its symbolic end — but the experience, of course, stays with me.

The quote *"It's not the destination, it's the journey"* is often attributed to American philosopher Ralph Waldo Emerson. While he apparently didn't use those exact words, he did write about the idea that it's the experience of life — not just the outcome — that truly matters. My *Everywhere* journey is perhaps the embodiment of that sentiment, and something I appreciated more as the kilometres rolled by.

I first came to Australia in 2001 on what was meant to be a six-week backpacking holiday. I'm still here. The journey continues — and the longer I stay and the more I see, the more I fall in love with this country.

While crazy things seem to be happening around the world, Australia feels comfortable in its own skin — a solidness and resilience built up over millennia. With challenging terrain and deadly risks on land and sea, it's not hard to see where that resilience comes from.

Along the way I've seen so many faces of Australia — from its ancient Aboriginal heritage, with stories and songlines stretching back tens of thousands of years, to the convict past etched into sandstone walls; from gold rush towns where fortunes rose and fell, to cities where beaches brush right up against the skyline; from endless outback roads and dusty tracks to rainforests dripping with life. I've wandered through country towns with wide verandahs, watched sunburnt paddocks roll on forever, and shared a beer in plenty of desert pubs. This journey has been a patchwork of all these places and stories — ancient, tough, beautiful, surprising, and uniquely Australian.

Of course, no country is perfect — or maybe it's that the land itself is perfect, and it's just the population still working toward that mythical endgame.

And perhaps that's the beauty of it: Australia isn't a finished product — it's a work in progress, just like the journey itself. And knowing this, it doesn't take itself too seriously.

And truth be told, despite my best efforts, I haven't really been everywhere — not yet, anyway. There are still many adventures waiting and plenty more miles to travel. So don't wait too long to start your own journey — this big, beautiful country is waiting.

Who knows, maybe we'll cross paths somewhere out there — in a dusty outback pub, on a beachside track… or humping a bluey on the dusty Oodnadatta Road.

A - Z INDEX

Town / Chapter

Adelong / 76

Augathella / 9

Ballarat / 86

Bambaroo / 12

Bangalow / 69

Bendigo / 87

Billabong / 78

Birdsville / 94

Boggabilla / 6

Boggabri / 52

Bouindarra / 21

Brigalow / 17

Brindabella / 27

Cabramatta / 49

Canberra / 28

Captains Flat / 29

Caringbah / 46

Casino / 71

Cloncurry / 11

Collaroy / 43

Condamine / 18

Coolangatta / 64

Cunnamulla / 8

Dalveen / 55

Dandenong / 84

Darwin / 91

Deniliquin / 88

Dorrigo / 72

Emmaville / 53

Engadine / 47

Ettalong / 23

Fingal / 66

Geelong / 85

Gin Gin / 14

Girraween / 51

Goondiwindi / 7

Grong Grong / 90

Gulgong / 34

Gundagai / 75

Gunnedah / 3

Indooroopilly / 62

Jerilderie / 77

Jindabyne / 30

Kilmore / 83

Kirribilli / 44

Kumbarilla / 16

Kurrajong /40

Kurri Kurri / 2

Lismore / 70

Lithgow / 38

Maroochydore /59

Megalong / 39

Milperra / 48

Mittagong / 26

Molong / 37

Mooloolaba / 60

Moree / 5

Morella / 10

Muckadilla / 20

Mullumbimby /68

Murwillumbah / 67

Nambour / 58

Narrabeen / 42

Narrabi / 4

Narromine / 35

Oodnadatta / 93

Parramatta / 50

Proserpine / 13

River Murray / 82

Seymour / 80

Stockinbingal / 74

Strathpine / 61

Tamborine / 65

Taree / 73

Terrigal / 1

Tibooburra / 92

Toowoomba / 57

Tuggerawong / 24

Tullamore / 36

Turramurra / 41

Ulladulla / 31

Unanderra / 32

Wallangarra / 54

Wallaville / 15

Wallumbilla / 19

Wanganella / 89

Wangaratta / 81

Wollondilly / 25

Wollongong / 33

Woodenbong / 56

Woolloomooloo / 45

Wyong / 22

Yarra Yarra / 79

Yeerongpilly / 63

AFTERWORD

If you're thinking of hitting the road to visit all those places in *I've Been Everywhere, Man*, I say go for it — it's a cracking adventure. But don't rush it. Take your time, stop and soak it all in... and while you're at it, take a break at one of Australia's legendary Driver Reviver stations.

On my run from Rocky down to Gin Gin, I came across my first Driver Reviver stop, where I met Peter (a Swedish exchange student, would you believe), along with locals Glenn and Ken. These three cheerful characters were only too happy to have a yarn and serve up a free coffee and a few bikkies.

I was especially impressed when Glenn mentioned he'd been to Bambaroo — that tiny dot on the Queensland map where pretty much the school *is* the town. And Peter, despite being from Sweden, spoke with an Aussie accent so thick you'd swear he'd spent his whole life in the outback. Classic.

When tackling long stretches, I make sure I pull up regularly for a stretch, and I'm not shy about having a good old nanny nap when I need to recharge. Honestly, there's no excuse not to — especially when you're passing through such interesting country.

Driver Reviver Tips for Travellers

For anyone planning their own lap of this wide brown land, here are a few wise words from the folks at Driver Reviver — their top tips for staying safe (and awake) on the road:

• Make sure you're well rested before heading off.

• Passengers should be rested too — no good having sleepy passengers when they could be helping navigate or entertain.

• Plan to stop at least every two hours; 15 minutes is a good break.

• Share the driving when you can and give your relief driver confidence.

• If you've got kids aboard, bring interesting things to keep them occupied.

• Research where you're headed and prepare a quiz — keeps everyone engaged.

• Watch the temperature inside the car so it doesn't get too cosy and send you off to sleep.

• Keep music at a pleasant, non-distracting level.

• Pack a picnic and a thermos — but no booze.

• Be flexible: if you're getting tired, don't wait — pull over and have a quick nap.

• If you catch yourself rubbing your eyes, that's your sign to stop.

So, if you're out there exploring, do yourself a favour: stop, stretch, have a yarn and grab a cuppa. And if you happen to pull in at the Driver Reviver near Rocky, say g'day to Peter, Glenn and Ken for me — top blokes.

Fun Fact:

The Driver Reviver program has been operating since 1989, with thousands of volunteers helping keep Aussie travellers safe by offering free tea, coffee and biscuits at rest stops.

Must See:

- Driver Reviver stations themselves — scattered across the country and usually staffed by friendly locals and volunteers with a story or two to tell.

Key statistics:

- Average duration between recommended breaks: 2 hours
- Number of Driver Reviver sites nationally: around 200 (seasonally operated)
- Cuppas served since program inception: millions — and probably a few thousand Tim Tams too!

ABOUT THE AUTHOR

Peter Harris is a writer, operator of an independent IT business and financial counsellor. Originally from the UK and now happily settled in Australia, Peter has spent decades helping people with financial troubles, running small businesses and occasionally wandering into places that don't always make the tourist brochures.

When not working, he can often be found travelling remote roads, unearthing curious histories, or quietly observing Australians' fondness for claiming 'the longest, tallest, biggest thing in the southern hemisphere'.

Peter's writing blends dry humour with a practical, honest take on life's inevitable ups and downs. He lives with his husband, Billy, and a thoroughly indulged Cavalier King Charles Spaniel named Lucy.

ALSO BY PETER C HARRIS

Your business will die and so will you.

ISBN 9781764143110

www.ingramcontent.com/pod-product-compliance
Lightning Source LLC
Chambersburg PA
CBHW071228070526
44583CB00017B/2094